# Journey in Grace

*In this journey of life,
Jesus Christ is the grace*

## GRACE MILLS

ISBN 978-1-64468-283-8 (Paperback)
ISBN 978-1-64468-284-5 (Hardcover)
ISBN 978-1-64468-285-2 (Digital)

Covenant Books, Inc.
11661 Hwy 707
Murrells Inlet, SC 29576
www.covenantbooks.com

# Dedication

This book is dedicated to my Lord and Savior Jesus Christ, my grace in this journey of life.

To Audrey, Alexis, and Snookum-nook.

# Special Appreciation

To my Pastor Andre Butler who woke me to the reality that I had a book in me.

To my friend Angie, Father God gave when my mother transitioned.

# Table of Contents

## CHAPTER 1

# The Journey Begins

My journey in grace started on a frigid January morning in 1961. I was the second child born to Harold and Patricia Mills. I had a birthmark over one of my eyes that disappeared by the time I became an adolescent. My grandmother told my mother it meant I would have some kind of special sight or purpose for my life. Whether birthmark or unique destiny, I am sure I was fearfully and wonderfully made by Father God for a purpose. My mother told me I was the only child that she attended church with every Sunday, during her pregnancy. She said it gave her peace, and she allowed her to ignore my father's drinking.

I don't know the details of how they met but I know how they ended up married. Not long into the courtship, my mother told me she and my father went on a date. He picked her up from my grandparents' house and dropped her off at a friend's. Somewhere between getting pizza and returning, he was arrested for being intoxicated. The next day, when he took my mother home, my grandmother asked, "When are y'all getting married?"

Whatever else transpired after that, they married shortly after. My brother, Harold, was born first. According to my mother, she never wanted me. She was content to have one son and wasn't interested in having any more children. I imagine she was well aware that her husband was an alcoholic, by that point. If she had had her way, I would have never been born, but—"Your father put a whole in the rubber." For as long as I could remember; whenever I made a mistake, whenever she was angry (which was often), whenever she was unhappy with her lot in life—she reminded me I wasn't wanted.

I don't know if what my mother told me about my father putting a whole in the condom was true. If it was, he showed me no preference as his only daughter. Although my parents did not welcome me into the world, my heavenly Father loved and welcomed me. Predestined before the foundation of the world, I am not a mistake, but on a divine assignment. Knowing that I am not a mistake, I am enlightened to God's love for me. While we were in sin, the Father sent His only Son to pay for our transgressions. Christ's sacrificial work at the cross cloaks me in righteousness and brings to the presence of the Father. Think about that for a moment. We are valuable to God! God created us in His image to His glory. Throughout my life, He is always present. Even in moments of tragedy, He has never left me. God provides life, and life is the journey.

Harold Mills Sr. was the only son born to Jessie and Gertrude Mills. Besides my father, they had two daughters. Jesse and Gertrude were simple people from the hometown of Harper Lee, Monroeville, Alabama. They came here to work for Ford, one of the few companies during the Depression that offered a livable wage. I never knew them to buy luxury or nonessential items. They never bought birthday or Christmas presents for their grandchildren.

My father's parents separated because my grandmother refused to live with Jesse's drinking and arguing. I venture to say, Gertrude Wiggins-Mills was the gustiest of all my elders. I didn't know much about her other than her father paid for her and her sister's education. She never spoke about her father. She was light-skinned, and she kept a photo of what appeared to be a white man.

Gertrude's father didn't approve of her marriage choice. He was not the same class or complexion as she was. Jesse was dark-skinned and his parents were sharecroppers. If you were black a light-skinned at that time, you married light, you married right. You didn't marry someone with less education and more melanin than you. When the first child born to that union had a dark complexion, she knew she could never return home.

Highly intelligent, my father was double-promoted and grad-uated at 16 from high school. My grandparents gave their consent for him to enlist in the military at seventeen years old. He started drinking and smoking early to fit in with his peers. He served in the Air Force as a registered nurse and was honorably discharged shortly before meeting my mother. Once they married, my father re-enlisted to provide for his family.

He was soft spoken and fairly laid back, so it doesn't surprise that he went along with the shotgun wedding. I never heard him raised his voice, but my mother contended when was drunk, he liked to fight. Ultimately the drinking and the fighting caused their sepa-ration, though they never divorced.

I remember he called my mother Tricia and he used to say "Tricia, I love you from the top of your head to the bottom of your butt." Although my parents separated shortly after I was born, my father was frequently present, though seemingly uninterested in his children. He never did any activities with us or spent time with me and my brother. In that way, he was much like his own father. They both drank. They both like to fight when they drank. In time, they would be companions, living under the same roof, drinking and fighting.

Eventually my mother met another man, Wilbur, with whom she had my sister, Pearl and youngest brother, Benjamin. He lived with us for a short time on Kitchener Street, but he was physically abusive, and my mother always prided herself in saying "I won't tol-erate no man hitting me." Decades later, I only have one memory of the guy, and he was mean.

One night, after entertaining guests, my mother left to take some people. He told me to go to bed, but I told him I wanted to wait up for my mother. I was no older than four years old. My refusal caused him to forget I was only a child or maybe he didn't care. He dragged me to my room, ripping my shirt in the process, and flung me into the bed.

In the spring of 1965, my youngest sister Pearl was born. I was four years old, living on Detroit's eastside with my mother and my brother, Harold. I can't imagine the mental and emotional state of my mother at the time. In retrospect, she may have a severe case of post-partum depression that exacerbated her psychological state of mind, but after the winter of 1965, I was never the same.

## CHAPTER 2

# The Winter of 1965

The Detroit News records the blizzard of February 1965 as the most brutal winter storm in the Midwest since December 1929. Everything was closed: schools, offices, shops, manufacturing plants. Street were barricaded by snow. The Lodge Freeway was an "automobile junkyard". Hospitals enlisted the help of anyone in the building, electricians, plumbers, janitors to help feed patients and perform non-medical care.

We were living in a two-family flat on Kitchener Street. My mother was in the upstairs flat, sitting with our neighbors. As the sun pierced the gauzy curtains, Harold and I played with matches in one of the bedrooms, where my sister Pearl was sleeping. We were lighting tissue paper on fire. It would burn with an orange glow, leaving a brown outline from the fire. The tissue burned so quickly—we were fascinated!

We watched the flames consume the tissue. As it got closer to our fingers, we and threw the tissue underneath the crib. However dangerous it was, we were playing, as kids do. Soon the scent of burning tissue made its way upstairs, to where our mother was.

My mother came downstairs in a fury! She screamed at us for playing with fire. She grabbed me first. "I'm gonna teach you a lesson." She took me in her lap and grabbed a cigarette lighter. It was from a matching lighter and ashtray set. It was a ceramic ashtray with a brown dog and puppies.

She held my hands to the flame and I shrieked.

"SHUT UP!"

I kept quiet as my flesh began to melt. It seemed like an eternity. Then she grabbed Harold and burned him, too. She didn't hold him as long. His burns were minor. Perhaps her rage subsided, maybe she finally woke to the horror that she had done. In any event, she stopped.

My mother burned all my fingers on both of my hands.

Some days later, my father came over. He bundled me up and carried me through waist-high snow to Jefferson Avenue, where he could catch a cab to take us to Children's Hospital. He never asked me what happened. I never overheard any argument or accusation of abuse from him. I don't remember how many surgeries I endured. I remember that nauseating black mask they put on my face before every operation to this day.

I got my first skin graft when I arrived at the hospital, which came from my right front thigh. I played with the other kids, completely ignoring the condition of my hands and the pain. Eventually my hands got infected, which led to gangrene. I lost the tip of my right index finger and received a second skin graft that came from my right inner forearm. In total, I received three skin grafts.

The hospital stays meant I had my mother's pleasant attention, if only for others' sake. She was always polite in front of others. Child abuse technically wasn't a crime in Michigan in 1965. Even if I could muster the courage to tell the nurses what she did, it was pointless.

On one of my father's visits, he taught me how to use my left hand to write. "You got two hands. While one wears bandages, you need to learn how to use the other hand." Eventually, with lots of practice, I learned to write and sign my name with both hands. Consequently, I have been ambidextrous most of my life.

Before this event, I don't think either of us knew about our mother's rage. The cigarette lighters disappeared after she burned us, but she kept the ashtrays for many years. I never to complained to her about my hands hurting because as she was burning me, she told me to shut up. I didn't understand why she did that to me, but I didn't hate her for it. I never hated her for it. As a child, I was desperate for her lo. How, how could I hate her?

## CHAPTER 3

# The Whitmore's

My mother was the youngest girl of eight children. Her parents were Emanuel and Callie Mae Whitmore. My grandmother was the first person I observed reading the Bible. She prayed on her knees every night. I believe she prayed for our family.

Callie Mae was an excellent saver. She sold Avon and worked for Wayne County in housekeeping till she retired. Never making much money, she managed it well and helped my mother whenever possible. She frequented the secondhand store on Mack Avenue and bought clothes for me and my siblings.

Emanuel was a spender. He and my brother, Harold, once got a settlement from an accident they were involved in. My father never provided much guidance, so of course, my teenage brother spent it all on material stuff. Surprisingly, my grandfather did the same. He couldn't work because of an accident that amputated his leg, but he got around pretty well with the prosthesis and cane.

My mother's parents were never kind to each other, and they grew old together that way before my grandfather passed. Emanuel verbally abused my grandmother, calling her a dumb dough roll: that was his favorite name for her. It sounded like "dumb doro". One day, my siblings and I were in the car with them when he called her that name for the umpteenth time. We heard her composed voice from the front passenger seat, "Emanuel, stop calling me that or I will hit you on your head with your cane." It sounds funny now, but I believe she meant to do it if he said it again. I think he believed her too because we never heard "dumb doro" again.

My mother told me that my grandfather was physically violent towards my grandmother, and once she left, but came back. The physical abuse stopped when my uncles became teenagers. She learned from her parents, particularly my grandfather, how to be mean and destroy the esteem of her children.

We had Sunday dinners at my grandparents' house. Occasionally, my cousins would be there, which made Sundays special because I got to see my aunts and uncles. My mother never came, but my grandparents always sent food to her. She never said why, but I could guess. It may come as some surprise—perhaps it won't—that no one ever asked me about my hands. She and I being in the same room might have been too big of an elephant to ignore. Between depression and other health issues, my mother struggled with her weight most of her life. Perhaps she just didn't like my grandmother calling her fat in front of the family.

My mother also thought her family resented her for leaving her husband and having two more children with another man. It was unheard of in the sixties, at least in my family culture. I wonder if it ever occurred to her, they may have experienced some inner conflict with what she did, even though no one said anything. Whether these things were true, it was her reality. She believed them, and we live out our beliefs.

My grandfather was frequently cruel to my mother. He once called Child Protection Services on my mother. Not for abuse, but because we had a dog. A social worker came to the house, peeking through the living room window. He made a false report that the dog was pooping in the house. The dog wasn't even allowed in the house.

My mother called Big Daddy, screaming obscenities. When she hung up, she told us not to answer the phone. The phone just rang all day. He just kept calling. Apparently, he didn't care no one was answering. I never understood why he provoked her like that. I'm sure he didn't antagonize my aunts in that manner.

One dispute resulted in her making us pack up all the clothes they gave us and hauling them in wagons, around the corner to their house. I remember I had to give up a pair of Levi jeans that fit perfect.

Any conflicts with my mother ended in being shunned. I had no one to teach me differently, so I believed I caused her anger and rejection. My sense of self-worth was miniscule. I wanted to go along to get along: anything to avoid rejection or annoying her. I did my best not to make any mistakes, of course I failed.

## ❧ CHAPTER 4 ❧

# *Childhood Life with Momma*

Outspoken, she titled herself the black sheep of her family. When I was young, I didn't know what that meant. Since she only said it in association with her misbehavior or her own feelings of rejection, I concluded black sheep were bad.

My mother was a pioneer of sorts. She was the first woman in her family to leave her husband (and not return). My father fought with my mother when he was drunk. My mother always said, "I can't tolerate a man hitting me." I assume this assertion came from not wanting to be like her mother, who returned to her husband to endure verbal abuse, in lieu of physical.

The irony that she abused me my entire childhood is not lost on me. As much as she fled abuse of the men in her life, she inflicted it on her children. As I got older, I had a hard time reconciling her philosophies with what I was experiencing. Was she somehow better or more valuable than me? Did I somehow deserve her treatment of me?

As with most children, my most defining relationship was with my mother. That relationship fashioned how I viewed myself and the world around me. My mother saw my birth as an intrusion: something forced on her.

Even after my mother had two other children, she didn't stop telling me she never wanted me. Additionally, I bore the resemblance of my father—a double offense. She was a voice inside my head that

10

delivered singular unworthiness. *I never wanted you. Your father put a hole in the rubber.* In my mother's eyes, no one was unwanted as I was.

With the burning of my hands, I thought it was a certainty that no one else would want me, either. It intensified my need for her acceptance. I don't think my mother was conniving enough to exploit my emotions in this manner, but I think it may have fed her own fears of rejections. I changed my behavior to satisfy her whims. I didn't retaliate like how my sister Pearl later learned to cope with my mother's abuse. When she was frustrated, I retreated to my room and the company of my birds.

## Cyclone

When we moved from Kitchener to Crane Street, my mother packed that ceramic dog ashtray and took it with us to the new house. Eventually, it disappeared. I don't know what happened to it.

I often thought about the meaning behind the mother dog and her whelps. The puppies were children chained to their mother. They served from time to time as reminders of the day my mother held me in her lap and disfigured my hands. My connection to her felt cemented, like those puppies molded into that ashtray with their mother.

The ashtrays disappeared from the living room when the glass menagerie appeared. It was a beautiful glass table with glass ornaments of all kinds: horses, fish, figurines—you name it.

My youngest brother entertained himself with the habit of throwing up baseballs in the air, and it didn't matter to him where he was. This little boy was playing ball in the vicinity of the glass figurines, and of course, the ball went up and came down on one of the tiny glass statues, and it broke. My mother came downstairs like a tornado, whipped the table over, smashing all the glass figurines, then demanded that we clean it up. Then she returned to her room and slammed the door. The beautiful glass menagerie was destroyed in a fit of rage, from my brother breaking one, by mistake.

On another occasion, my youngest brother, Ben, accidentally set my mother's bed on fire. There were no violent outbursts. I was surprised. He was in my mother's room, playing with matches. I was sleeping in my bedroom when I was awakened by my mother yelling for me to stop teasing my brother. Confused, I stumbled out of bed, half asleep. My mother had just doused the mattress with a bucket of water. In silence, she took it out of the house. Then she cried. That scared me.

"I don't want this for you," showing him my hands, reminding him what happened to me.

My mother's outburst of anger for mistakes was a lesson in conditional love and acceptance. I thought if I was good enough, maybe I could earn her favor. What I didn't know was you can't merit love. Prayer changed things in the house. I was always asking God to help my mother.

Her erratic behavior shaped my ability to function in relationships. The message was if you don't like what someone says, just throw them away. The bond only serves to affirm your perspective on things. It's a mindset of self-centeredness. The only emotion I experienced from her was anger.

Violence has an energy that didn't feel good. Even if I wasn't the object of that anger. Anger made the whole environment heavy. No words were spoken. A loud silence filled the house. Once the eruption was finished, the tension seemed to last for weeks. There was no resolution to the conflict, leaving a sense of unfinished discord in the air waiting to re-erupt. The volatile atmosphere stole any semblance of peace. There was no escaping it. I often retreated to my bedroom to pray, frequently crying myself to sleep.

Not only were they triggered by minor mistakes, but sometimes when I braced for a tirade, she laughed! Once I broke a shampoo bottle. Johnson and Johnson just started making plastic bottles. The label said it was "unbreakable." I decided to test the statement. So, I dropped it, and it didn't break. I hit it against the wall. Again, it didn't break. I stomped it with my foot, and it exploded! I was terrified. Shampoo was everywhere. I was in trouble now!

I took the busted shampoo bottle to my mother. Her response surprised me. I could tell she was angry at first, but my uncle was visiting. She laughed and asked, "Why did you do this?" I told her the bottle said it was unbreakable. She said you can't believe everything you read. It seemed other adults influenced her mood and behavior. In this case, I was grateful, but I wondered why.

All this confusion and chaos took place with a Bible open on the living room coffee table. It was more of a religious decoration than an instrument of worship. I never witnessed my mother read God's word, nor was there a time she talked to us about God or Jesus Christ.

I believe His open word protected us during the confusion. The bible on the coffee table somehow spoke of His grace. All of us in that house God loved.

## Suicide Attempts

Occasionally, my mother tried to kill herself during the winter holidays. Once she filled the house with gas from the oven. She put towels underneath our bedroom doors; I guess in an attempt to spare our lives. Apparently, she didn't consider the gas could have caused an explosion that killed everyone in the house. She must've called a suicide hotline because the police were dispatched to the house. We awoke to the Detroit Police kicking in the front door.

When she refused to talk to them, they wrestled her onto her bed and arrested her. The abuse that was already going on brought more brutality from the outside. After that, she never called anyone or used the stove in any other suicide attempts. Another time, she took pills, but she only fell out of bed and busted her chin. Another time, she slashed her wrist and received more stitches.

One time when she and I were alone in the house, she jumped off the two-story back porch. She landed in the dirt and had a few scrapes and bruises. When I went downstairs to open the back door, she quietly crawled in. I went back to my bedroom and cried. Who would take care of us if something happened to her? I felt helpless. Despite the abuse, I was afraid of being abandoned. I prayed, "God, please make my mother better. Help her." Eventually stopped attempting suicide.

The end of her suicide attempts brought new kinds of abuse, capitalizing on the same old fears: abandonment. She would say, "I'm going to leave and never come back." One evening, she put on this pretty purple outfit she made and left it. I cried and prayed she would come back. I don't know how long she was gone. I cried myself to sleep, but she was back by the morning. Later, she told us she just took a walk.

Our mother's abrupt actions were always followed by her saying, "You better not go to grandma and granddaddy's." One day during summer vacation, Ben, Pearl, and I spent the day building a house in the yard with doors and plywood we found in the neighborhood. We were never given a reason, but I assume she was aggravated by the opening and slamming of the door as we came in and out of the house. She locked us out of the house without warning. My siblings were visibly shaken up by the situation. The immediate concern was access to a bathroom and food. We knew not to go around the corner to our grandparent's. When Harold came home, he didn't let us in for fear of being put out. He fed us tuna sandwiches on toasted bread with a slice of tomato.

I developed a self-sufficient personality as I approached adolescence. Of course, I understood the legal system wouldn't allow a child to live without adult supervision, and I knew nothing of being emancipated. Of course, my mother wouldn't allow anything that meant less welfare. But I began to understand that one day I would be free from my mother's confusion.

Still, I thought, what made me so different from my brother? She seemed to adore him. There was a place of love and acceptance in her heart, but I couldn't seem to locate it or gain egress. I tried to do everything right, but it seemed he could do no wrong. It was an example of unconditional love, and that love existed in my mother for someone. Why not me?

Nevertheless, my siblings and I had good times with my mother. There were occasional glimpses of another woman that surfaced: accepting, generous, funny, and creative. My siblings and I made cots on the floor in her room: the only room in the house with an air conditioner. In those times, I imagined our lives could've been different.

## Talented Seamstress

My mother was a magnificent seamstress. She could make anything with or without a pattern. She stayed up all night making outfits for special occasions: for school field trips, cruises, weddings. She even made my daughter's prom dress. Crocheting was a favorite pastime of hers. All her children and grandchildren received afghans from her. Her gifts are precious to my family to this day.

My mother would make costume jewelry and sew for people for extra money until she realized people didn't want to pay her for her time or her talents. The electricity for the sewing machines costs money. Making aprons appeared to be a more straightforward process; it required no fitting or measuring, just a finished product to sell. She was always generous with us with the little money she made.

On one occasion, a lady commissioned my mother to make a dress; however, she wanted my mother to purchase a pattern that wasn't her size. Either my mother couldn't explain to her she wasn't or wouldn't do it. That situation turned into this lady calling the house and cussing out whoever answered the phone until my little brother answered the phone. He cussed her out in return; it was amusing a little boy with a deep voice she never called back again.

## Early Faith

Whether I was six or sixteen, I don't remember. I saw, not by physical eyesight, but by inward sensing, whatever someone else was. At an early age, I was inquisitive and fascinated to explore by reading. That gift of curiosity was given to me by Father God. Since the Word of God is alive, every time I looked at it, I experienced hope that's difficult to explain. My heart knew things my mind was yet to understand.

This sensing, as I reflect, wasn't my intellect. The Holy Spirit's presence articulated something in me beyond what I could not understand by my five senses. Once Father God comes, no matter your age, He comes to stay. He declares, "I will never leave you" (Hebrews 13:4).

Reading the Bible in the living room intrigued me. This book wasn't an ordinary book; it spoke to me. The Word of God is alive, and it speaks. It is God speaking to the believer.

The bible was always open to Psalms. Psalms is the middle of the Bible. David, a man after God's heart, speaks of God being mighty and having mercy. The book of Proverbs followed Psalms. Proverbs became my favorite book. They were short sayings of consequences, not immediate, but imminent. God's wisdom for every occasion and situation.

My introduction to Jesus Christ gave clarity. I knew I was here on purpose, for a purpose, with a goal. This was the beginning of my journey to see the grace of Jesus Christ. God made man for prospering from the very beginning. In Genesis 1:27, God blessed man. In Joshua 1:8, He told Joshua to talk about and meditate-think on the law day and night to observe; then you will make your way prosperous and have success if God didn't want the man to prosper. Why? Would He say so! Why does He tell the man how? Jesus said in Matthew 5:17, "Do not think that I came to destroy the Law or the Prophets. I did not come to destroy but fulfill". Jesus is our meditation under the New Testament, not the law. The sensing had to come from the Holy Spirit, since nothing in my environment gave me a reason to believe for better days.

Although all books had information, they didn't all speak to me—the determination to understand things fueled its way into a litany of questions. I would ask my mother questions, and she gave me books to read. The more I read, the more questions I had. Eventually, my mother told me to stop asking questions. It didn't deter my curiosity.

A sense like I knew there is a God, a higher power that cares about me and my life. Every time I prayed, things changed for a while, and that gave way to belief. Every time I prayed, even a simple prayer, something good happened. That gave me a sense of connection to the knowledge that God is real.

Although most of my Bible reading didn't yield a great deal of understanding, I felt like everything God did was a completed act. God made man and woman complete. He made the herbs, animals for food and clothes, fruits, and vegetables of all kinds (Genesis 11:1). God blessed them to multiply and fill the earth. Nowhere, in Genesis, does God speak of man being sick. I concluded God didn't make sickness. So why was my mother ill? She was always suffering from some ailment. I thought, does God not care about my mother?

But my mother was always overcoming some health challenges. The medicines the doctors were prescribing her weren't yielding her to a state of better health. There were times she would be tired for what seemed like days or weeks from the pills the doctors had prescribed her, never emerging from these states in a better frame of health or mind. During the times of my mother's incapacitation, Harold made sure we ate and assisted our mother in writing checks, shopping, or anything else that was needed.

My mother's state of health influenced me to read books about vitamins, herbs, and plants. God made everything, right?! I wanted to understand why things were happening in my life and family. I believe the answer was somewhere in a book. The Bible wasn't providing an understanding of the daily events of my life that I could see. I saw life instructions: Honor your mother and father for your days to belong on the earth. Proverbs provided predictability and immediate consequences for behavior and actions.

My mother wasn't a churchgoer. But occasionally, we would go to church with a neighbor. Seldom did she speak of Jesus Christ or God, and when she did, it was in a tone of betrayal saying things like, "Why did God let these things happen to me" followed by "I just want to die." I didn't understand why there was a Bible on the coffee table in the living room. Whether this was an item of decoration or religious worship, I don't know.

I read a book titled "How to be Assertive," the author I can't recall. The book was small and white with only words on the cover. This book's title moved me to read it and to capture the significance of assertiveness in my personality.

The dictionary was a world of words. Inside each word are several other words, which led to different meanings. The dictionary fascinated me. Words are receptacles. Inside each word is another term. It taught me several ways to say one thing. I couldn't read a book without a dictionary. There were always new and unfamiliar words to learn.

The dictionary gave assertive a description of boldness, ambition, and healthy self-esteem. Self-esteem meant having self-respect, confidence, which was synonymous with pride, egotistical—a direction I didn't need to go. Still, in my ignorance from an intelligence standpoint, I needed to think and feel good about myself. Something I didn't have. I viewed my hands as ugly, and so I considered myself also ugly. There is only one book that points humanity to beauty, and that is the Bible.

## Home Life

The spirit of rage that seemed to possess my mother would reign in the house. An environment of turmoil has a way of devaluing everyone present. The verbal rants addressed at one of us affected all of us.

My mother received little emotional support from her family. Of all her six siblings—one uncle and one aunt—consistently made themselves available, taking us on day trips or summer vacations. I observe my mother on more than one occasion, call her mother and get off the phone in a worse state, than when she got on it. When she got off the phone she was always crying. Not knowing what was said didn't seem as important as my mother's emotional state when she got off the phone. I was concerned about what was getting ready to happen to us! I grew to resent my grandmother, observing these reoccurring events. It never ended on a positive note for us.

I started Nichols Elementary School in the historical area of Indian Village. The area surrounding the school appeared to be another world. However, it was only two blocks away from where I lived. I would take different routes to school to see all the beautiful homes in the area. It fueled my imagination, and I wondered about the people that lived there, their style of decoration, and what type of furniture they had. The lawns were always well-manicured. Walking to school was a peaceful place. I dreamed of living there. It was always quiet and peaceful.

Going to school was bittersweet. I hated the teasing: I enjoyed walking to school and learning. All phases of school, from elementary to high school, brought new stages of change.

The peer pressure of each level yielded changes in my personality—coping skills or defense mechanisms for the rejection that happened during maturing. I learned to appreciate my own company, making me free of the opinion of others. My years of adolescence were a transitional period.

My oldest brother took care of all of us, including our mother. I couldn't imagine how he managed. I respected him then, and even more now. He was the glue that held us together. And as awful as it was, at least we were together and not in the foster care system. He carried the weight of the entire family. Being the oldest in this situation had no privileges other than being the first to be able to leave.

When I prayed for her and us, that would calm things down for a while. I just wanted her to stop hurting herself and us. What I didn't understand was she was caring for herself the same way she cared for us.

She would say she was tired of living. I don't doubt with no help from our fathers that being a single parent of four children was difficult. It appeared as if they went on with their lives as if we didn't exist. There were no child support payments made by either of them: only a welfare stipend for us to survive.

My mother was often sick, from kidney infections to mental depression. She was frequently in and out of hospitals. When she stayed at the hospital, my father would come over so there would be an adult present. That was all he was, an adult in the house. He still took part in libations as if he wasn't tending to us. Our grandparents lived close, but they didn't want to keep us for those stays.

## The Decision to Fight by Not Fighting

Whether this was a decision out of fear or divine influence, I'm not sure. I don't remember where I was or what I was doing when I came to understand that fighting didn't solve issues. I would not battle at school and at home. More to the point, I wouldn't fight with my sister anymore. I can't say this was a position of being brave or foolish. It wasn't giving me a pleasant outcome at home. At school, it was a no-brainer; I had to defend myself for the appearance of my hands or at least I thought so. To come to these types of conclusions wasn't me but the grace of God.

Shortly after I concluded that I would not fight at home, the occasion arose where my sister hit me. I refused the challenge. I push her away and told her, "I'm not fighting, leave me alone!" I don't remember what the disagreement was about, and it didn't matter. I can't remember what most of our conflicts were about other than they always resulted in a physical altercation that solved nothing. I think it was her way of handling our environment of confusion and chaos.

Although I couldn't anticipate my sister's response to my new position, and I didn't care. The fighting thing wasn't working for me. Refusing to engage wasn't good enough for her. After the initial push and request for her to leave me alone, she tore off my shirt and scratched my face and neck. With no further response from me, she left me alone.

When our mother came home, she asked, "What happened to you?" I told her Pearl did it. She asked me why I let her do that to me and I told her I wasn't fighting my sister, whatever the disagreement. I couldn't tell my mother I couldn't fight at home and school, because kids teased me about my hands at school. We never spoke about my hands.

My mother chastised me for not fighting back. She whipped Pearl, and that took care of the fights between us from that point on. That was a relief, but I got teased by my siblings for tattling. I didn't care; that ended my fighting at home. Looking back on that event, I realize it could've only been the Holy Spirit. I wasn't smart enough to think or know the outcome of the decision to stop fighting my sister. My sister and I were like night and day, but she was my sister. I felt we needed each other somehow, regardless of our differences.

The forms of abuse changed as we grew up. The older we became, the method of control changed. My sister had no problem defending herself against our mother. My youngest brother Ben and

I didn't fight our mother; we learned to escape. My oldest brother, after being checked by our Uncle Jay, he wasn't aggressive toward my mother. He learned avoiding my mother was best. It was interesting that there was no one to check her about how she treated us. I'm sure other family members knew, but either they didn't care or didn't know what to do.

My hands, in my mind, made me ugly. I felt my hands got noticed before anything else; I put my whole personality in my hands. I retreated from people and became an observer. The effects of childhood are far-reaching beyond the years of childhood development. The most unfortunate part was I developed minimal communication skills. Communication is more than asking for what you want; it's also about listening and reading a situation. I understood anger real well, but few other emotions.

## Seeking Sanctuary and Escape

Being inquisitive led me to want to play an instrument. First, one of my uncles loaned me his baritone. It was too big for me to handle. I would stand at the music classroom door to observe what musical instrument I could play comfortably. I noticed the trombone. It was perfect. I didn't need all my fingers, and I liked the tone and pitch.

I thought maybe I could make my mother proud. The music teacher denied me the opportunity to play any instrument in elementary school; I don't remember his reason. When I got to junior high, that music teacher allowed me in the music class. I would practice for hours; this was a new escape.

Although I was a girl and most trombone players were boys playing, there wasn't any negative scrutiny. I stumbled into a place where my hands got no attention, and I could relax in the company of others.

My grandparents helped my mother purchase a horn for me: first a rental, then they bought me one, still a prized possession. When I got to high school, I played in the orchestra, marching band, and jazz band. The orchestra performed twice per year, and my mother attended the concerts. The jazz band played for two local television stations channels 56 and 62. My mother was proud of me, and so were my siblings. That was a grand moment!

My bedroom was my sanctuary, a small corridor-shaped space where I could imagine I was some place peaceful. I shared this space with four parakeets that flew around the room all day, and at night retreated to their cage, where I would cover them for the night. Although I didn't have a traditional door on my bedroom, they didn't fly out of the room. My mother put a soft accordion-type closure in the doorway for dressing in private.

My trombone practicing never seemed to bother the birds. They just kept on singing. My mother appreciated all kinds of music, so she would allow me to practice for hours from time to time. I hid and entertained myself in my room. Venturing outside my room meant being uncomfortable. One of the phrases used to describe my hands was the "five fingers of death." I refuse to cry in front of my teasers, but in my room, I could cry and listen to my birds sing. I imagined they were singing a song for me.

I didn't see myself as a suitable playmate. I had no friends: playing with others would spark curiosity about what happened to my hands, and I didn't want to explain. Explaining would involve talking about my mother burning my hands. The pain involved in saying my mother put them in fire always ended with me wanting to cry. I was most comfortable avoiding the conversation altogether.

It was far too painful for me to use my creative ability to lie. The pain would surface with the mere mentioning of what happened to your hands. What happened to my hands? It seemed to ring in my ears, then burn in my heart, and immediately my eyes would water.

Withdrawing became a safe place for me; no one could see me cry or look at my ugly hands. The condition of my hands affected my self-image, which affected my ability to socialize with others. Retreating and isolating felt better than being in an environment where someone felt like they needed to know what was going on with my hands. I kept my hands in my pockets at school or wore gloves, when possible, to minimize attention.

My mother's room was adjacent next to mine. I could frequently hear her at night, crying and talking to herself, or praying when the house was quiet. Whatever she was doing, she sounded distressed. I could sense her pain. Although I couldn't see it and neither could I understand it, but I wanted to. My mother wasn't one to share her feelings. She kept all things to herself except her rage.

## Family

I read a series of books on birth order and position. I gained an understanding of being the middle child. They are classic negotiators and peacemakers, sometimes serving as buffers. In my case, I was the praying type of buffer in the family. The middle child never has a unique position in the family. They are not the oldest who have all the parents' attention, and they are not the youngest in the family.

The middle child is born into a group. With family position and birth order, each child born is born into a different family. The family my oldest brother was delivered into wasn't the same family I was born into for every child born changes the dynamics.

The youngest in the family is often catered to by other family members. That attitude doesn't change in the workplace, marriage, and parenting. As I read the books on birth order and position, I could see how, even in the chaos, there was a sense of order.

My younger brother, Ben, cried a lot when he was young, but with time he stopped crying as much, or he learned how to mask it. He and I developed a special relationship because he too, heard "I never wanted you" from our mother. He didn't get the privilege of being the baby in the family but was assigned a place of disdain. My mother and Pearl, both the youngest in the family, bore similar traits. Both had to have their way, regardless of what it meant.

Being the oldest in our family environment meant being more than a big brother. He was a surrogate father. As I mentioned before, Harold was a part of a small settlement when he and our grandfather were involved in a car accident. The money elevated him to the official position of the man of the house. He brought our mother a fur

23

collar coat, as well as a few things for himself. There was no mention of saving or investing.

This first settlement (I say first settlement because there were others) hurt my brother beyond not making sound financial decisions. Money gave him a position none of us understood, but he enjoyed it. He became another person with money. He was obsessed with clothes, changing his outfit several times before leaving the house.

# Fathers

Although my father abused my mother, he never hit us. He functioned under the influence of alcohol. He finished nursing school with ease, but he couldn't keep a job. He lived with his father; both were alcoholics. They fought with each other when they were drunk.

The first man in my mother's life didn't protect her, as a father should. Instead, he was a cruel jokester or a mean person; neither trait isn't admirable for a father's position or role.

The father is the first leader, provider, teacher, and protector. Fathers set the standard for relationships with others, both inside and outside the home. The father and the mother are pillars of the child's emotional development. The father demonstrates the male role and sets the tone for an acceptable standard of treatment; if he's loving and gentle, she will look for those qualities in a man. However, if he is absent, as my father was, this journey to find meaningful male companionship becomes more challenging.

The purpose of a father starts with his wife: The husband loves his wife as Christ loved the church and gave himself for it, that he might sanctify and cleanse it with the washing of the water of the Word. Men are to love their wives as their bodies. He that loves his wife loves himself, the position and authority of the father as the head of the family is expressly assumed and sanctioned in the scriptures, as a likeness of Father God. If a father can provide his child or children with unconditional love, life becomes a smoother journey.

As I know my Heavenly Father, how much he loves me and is ever providing for me, my life becomes less stressful. When Father God says in his word, cast all my cares on him, that's what he means. He cares about every area of my life. I pray in confidence, knowing Father God hears me, not because I am good. I'm not, but because I am the righteousness of God in Christ Jesus.

The love of my Heavenly Father for me; God so loved the world that he gave his only begotten Son, Jesus Christ so that I can be reconciled to him. There is no greater love than the love of The Heavenly Father.

# Harold

My older brother was the first to exercise his freedom of choice. He played football, and that brought popularity. That popularity attracted girls. The girls gave sex, and with that came a new attitude. Our mother never talked to us about sex; she gave us books instead. I don't think she knew how to talk about sex or relationships. Why else would she marry a man she went on one date with that got drunk and went to jail.

Giving rise to more confusion, my mother did not know how to handle this developing young man. He no longer came straight home from school. One evening, he came home late, and our mother grabbed a fist full of hangers and started hitting him, with little response. She stopped hitting him and ignored him, using us as her messengers.

She passed messages through the rest of her children, "Tell your brother to do..." When we weren't around, she wrote notes. She refused to talk to him because she couldn't control him. He was a young man. I think he rather liked the silent treatment. He seemed not to be disturbed by the ordeal, and he did as she asked.

For Harold's sex education, she gave him a box of condoms and a book. It was no surprise when he had his first child before he finished high school. My mother asked, "What happened to the condoms?" He told her he gave them to his friend Vince, who coincidentally, already had a baby.

The situation seemed like a big deal to me, but not to my mother. She was calm about the whole thing. I was confused. I witnessed my mother tear the house up, looking for a piece of costume jewelry, a cameo pendant that disappeared. She accused us of stealing it and trashed the house.

Here was a baby, a person, and it seemed somewhat trivial to her. The girl's parents felt he should marry her; my mother disagreed. Ten years later, history repeated itself with my youngest brother, Ben.

I learned from watching this situation unfold; it communicated what is accepted will become an unspoken standard. The Bible on the living room table and the visits to the Kingdom Hall gave me a sense of religion: neither spoke of man's worth nor the love of God for man.

Each of us was worth much more than what was happening. The older we got; the forms of abuse changed from physical to mental. When we became teenagers, it turned into psychological manipulation. The violence that happened to one of us happened to all of us.

## CHAPTER 5

# Aunt Audrey: Divine Orchestration

God will provide an escape.
—1 Corinthians 10:13

Aunt Audrey was one of my mother's older sisters. She went to Wilberforce University and worked for the Veterans Administration. From what I could see, she lived well. I know now God gave me favor with my aunt. She had no kids of her own, but she had plenty of nieces and nephews besides me. She could have chosen anyone else to share her life with, but she chose me! I didn't know why Aunt Audrey invited me to visit her during the summer months, but I was glad she did!

She bought me the current Chicago fashion for school. It made me feel special. No one had blouses like mine! Spending time with my aunt showed me a new possibility for life.

Aunt Audrey lived in a small house in Zion, Illinois. I took my first plane ride to get there. A flight attendant was assigned to look after me was nice. I was the only child flying alone. For the first time, I felt like I mattered. I was important!

My aunt had a roommate, Ms. Cook, who operated a day-care business out of the house. There was a sense of solitude there: I never heard the neighbors. In the mornings, Ms. Cook delivered the Chicago Sun Times newspaper before picking the kids up for daycare. My aunt went to work, and I spent the day with Ms. Cook, helping with the kids' activities.

My imagination was stimulated by going to a different place and seeing a different life. Aunt Audrey was nothing like my mother. I never saw her blow up or heard her raise her voice. I felt safe there.

I explored the area and embraced the possibility of a new reality once I left home. I didn't miss Detroit once. How could I miss a place I didn't consider home? My first stay that summer was only about two weeks. It felt like it was over in the blink of an eye. Getting back on the plane back to Detroit smothered me with immense sadness.

Knowing my mother and aunt left the same home and chose different paths marked a new beginning of hope. I understood childhood was for a season—not forever. I could create my own home when I grew up. There was a clock winding down on my childhood. Getting away from my mother wouldn't happen at the stroke of midnight on January 27, 1979, but one day, I would be an adult and free from her rage.

My aunt moved to an apartment complex with a swimming pool in Waukegan. I taught myself to swim by spending time at the pool and watching others swim. In Waukegan, there were a lot of fields and undeveloped marshy areas. For a city kid, it was a land of discovery, a place for all-day explorations. It brought the reality of my nature books to life. I liked science: my favorite thing was my microscope. I examined everything: water, bugs, grass, tree bark, and whatever else I could find outside, the invisible and the tiny. The fields always provided something new to discover.

One day, I caught a frog, and my aunt let me keep it overnight in a glass container. He kept jumping and hitting the top of the container throughout the night. The following morning, I returned him to the pond. I found a bike frame in the trash. I asked my aunt for tires and rode all over Waukegan riding that makeshift bike.

My aunt also took me to visit my Uncle Emanuel in Los Angeles. The plane ride was much longer than Detroit to Chicago. We even went to Disneyland. It was like a dream! The Matterhorn was the most memorable ride for me.

My aunt instructed me to drink from the water dispenser instead of the faucet water and showed me why. She placed the tap water in a white dish. I could see tiny black or brown particles floating around. My aunt was always patient with me, showing me instead of telling me to gain my compliance.

One summer, I couldn't visit with my aunt because I needed surgery on my hands. That was the summer she was going to take me to the Bahamas. At the time, I had no idea what the Bahamas were, but I knew it meant not being on Crane Street.

She told me only a few things I remember well. Don't get credit cards and run them up: you're paying to use someone else's money. She was the first person to teach me anything about money. She also said don't let some boy tell you he loves you to have sex with you, because boys will say anything to get in your pants. That was the conversation about my sex education; my mother gave me a book.

I prayed for the chance to stay in Illinois and attend school. The answer to that prayer came on one summer when Detroit public school teachers went on strike. My mother allowed me to stay and enroll at St. Anastasia, a Catholic school in Waukegan. Aunt Audrey was always considerate of me: my feelings, what I wanted to eat, what I thought. The opportunity to live with my aunt, along with attending school, gave me a new perspective. She provided environmental and emotional stability. She didn't cuss or criticize me when I made a mistake, and she never told me I was worthless.

Before attending St. Anastasia, hanging around other kids was not a part of school life. In Waukegan, at a predominately white Catholic school, I was a new kind of different. Kids didn't tease me because my hands were ugly. Here I was black: I got teased for my skin color, facial features, and hair, but that didn't bother me. I wasn't the only black kid in the school. I gravitated toward other black kids, cast out for our common difference. Here I found acceptance.

I only attended from September to December. In December, I returned to Detroit for what I thought was a visit. Instead, I had to stay and finish the school year in Detroit. The private school experience was over.

My aunt was a Jehovah's Witness and took me to the Kingdom Hall on Sundays. During the week, we studied the New World Translation Bible at one of the brother's or sister's homes. At twelve, I did not know the bible was written in diverse languages, and there were many translations. I never become a Witness. The Jehovah's Witness religion had structure, but no warmth. I didn't care what my aunt's religion was. She cared about me and spent time with me: I felt loved!

My aunt enrolled me in summer day camp programs to visit museums in downtown Chicago. I enjoyed the Museum of Science and Industry most because there was an exhibit of the human body with all internal organs. It is fascinating to see what God made! For my first concert, Aunt Audrey bought tickets to see the Jackson 5. I think it was at Chicago's Amphitheater. I remember there was a girl a few rows back that screamed through the entire show!

I believe it was during my exposure to these new experiences: the kids, the school, and the suburban influence that I learned I could ignore people, or I could fight, but I couldn't beat everybody. Besides, I didn't like fighting. My stays with my aunt were brief, but they impacted my future. She showed me there was more to life than where I was living.

## CHAPTER 6

# *Coming of Age*

One night, I told my mother I didn't want to live with her anymore! She grabbed me and threw me in the car. I had no idea where she was taking me! I was scared! We arrived at the Wayne County Youth Home, the kiddy jail, located on East Forest Street, in Detroit, where my grandmother used to work. She said, "Well, you can stay here," pointing at the youth home. I immediately apologized; I didn't want to be locked up in a youth home. That night, as cruel as the act was, I learned my mouth could land me in places I have no desire to go or be.

However, when the Wayne County Sheriff's Department hired me, I learned my mother couldn't just drop me off at a youth home because I made her angry.

My time with my aunt transitioned into staying in Detroit and working. Youth enrichment was what it was called. There was little enrichment. According to Merriam Webster, the term enrichment means to make fruitful or more productive, especially by adding or increasing some desirable quality, attribute, or ingredient. I learned little from the city's enrichment program; it seemed more of an opportunity for it to gain labor at a minimal fee.

The first summer I worked for maybe a few days. It was insane: a group of city kids cutting down weeds in vacant lots all over the city under a sweltering sun with minimal breaks. After a few days, I said later for that work business and quit. My mother asked me why and

I told her I have the rest of my life to work. She said, "Well, I guess you won't have clothes for school." If that's all I was working for, I didn't need to work, but I didn't dare say that.

When my father came over, he asked the same question. I told him the same thing. He laughed and nodded as if he agreed and walked away. My mother could've convinced me to work had she asked, but having clothes was a non-motivator. Sure, I liked new things, but they weren't enough for me to work like a convict for slave wages.

When I was in the tenth grade, I had a friend named Tee. Mr. Moore, our history teacher suggested she apply for Wayne State University's summer program, Upward Bound. She thought it would be a great way to hang out without our mothers' interference, so we applied together. It was a summer program, how many academic requirements could it have?

I applied with little enthusiasm. Tee was smarter than I was. She was studying trigonometry, and I was barely passing basic math. She was a much better candidate than I was. I wasn't even sure I would be accepted.

To my surprise and dismay, I got into the program, and she didn't. I didn't want to go without her, but my mother encouraged me to go, so I went. Tee and I weren't friends after that. Perhaps, Tee was a part of a divine orchestration for me to submit for a program that I didn't know existed. Where this favor came from could've only been one person; it was Father God, not my idea, not my plan, not my goodness.

Around the age of sixteen, I realized I was a young woman with no clue about my role as a lady. I had no girlfriends to share social experiences with. I was clueless about what was acceptable or unacceptable. In the span of a few years, I would be free from my mother's custody, but I was also filled with uncertainty. I was elated, and I was also afraid at the same time. Everything I knew was about to change. I was leaving chaos for the unknown.

Adolescence shepherded me to adulthood with little to miss about my present and past. I had no one to nurture me into womanhood. The gift of time had brought me to a new bridge of liberty, freedom, and independence.

I set my attention on being noticed by the opposite sex. I thought that would be the closest thing to experiencing love. I heard what my aunt said, but I didn't know what love looked like, so how could I tell a trick to misuse me from the truth? Between my aunt's scant advice and my mother's book, neither gave me enough to make a quality decision. I had no sense of worth to dictate quality decision-making.

My father wasn't available to teach me because of his sickness. My father never told me I was pretty. I received no special treatment as "daddy's little girl". The first man in my life taught me how unavailable men could be. By the time I became an adult, I developed a feeling of indifference toward him.

As an adult, I had freedom, but no guidance. My home environment, void of conflict and confusion, yielded no direction. It was a place for surviving the day. Discussions of the future never took place. Your occupation was a job, not something you aspired to be.

I liked the idea of building, maybe going into architecture. On one of my visits to Illinois, I met a woman architect. I was impressed by her and thought it would be great to make houses like the ones I used to see on my walks to school. But I was never good at math and my counselor advised me I would need strong math skills to study architecture.

I treated that weakness in the same way as an emotionally painful issue: I avoided it. I knew nothing about tutors and didn't think to pray about my future. The counselors weren't there for guidance, although that's what their title was: guidance counselor.

I thought the alternative to serving people was to be a police officer. I liked the idea that law enforcement provided security and predictably; I was incorrect in my thinking. More on that later.

## Marcus: The First Courtship

In October 1978, Pearl introduced me to a well-dressed guy, named Marcus. He had beautiful teeth and a smooth, dark complexion. He had a soft voice and a laid-back way about him. My father had this laid-back way about him, too. In retrospect, the parallels between the two are undeniable.

Marcus was a streetwise neighborhood guy, about as fit for adulthood as I was. When he took me to meet his family for the first time, the event was an early warning sign that I slept on. His father, the deacon of a church, said to me, "They need to open up Alcatraz and put all my sons in there, cause ain't none of them any good and all my daughters are whores." I thought he was joking. I learned later he wasn't.

One of the first things Marcus gave me was Peabo Bryson's *Crosswind* album. The song "I'm So into You" quickly became his words in my mind. Being seventeen, romantic fantasy came easy. I listened to that song to the point of meditation.

Since Marcus fashioned himself as a deacon's son, I thought he was well versed in things of the Bible. Our time together quickly turned into Bible study. Our Bible studies focused on my role as a woman, never touching on his role. I thought surely if the Bible had a part for me, it had a section for him also! It became obvious rather quickly, the intent of the studies was to establish control. These biblical discussions led to me read and study scriptures independently. I attended a church on the corner of McClellan and Marietta. There was lots of singing, very little scripture reading. I needed to learn, not sing.

My mother didn't care for Marcus, so between work and school, my opportunities to see him were minimal. My mother provided supervision but no guidance. When I asked her why she didn't like him, she said, "He's too dark, and he won't look me in my eyes." She never explained the importance of eye contact. Had my mother taken the time to articulate her thoughts instead of making demands, it might have created a dialogue between him and me that could have changed our relationship. He gave me eye contact, that's all that mattered.

There was another warning, early in the relationship, when I failed to see Marcus for who he was. One evening, he came to visit, and I fell asleep. Shortly after he left, Ben noticed one of his necklaces was missing. Marcus was the prime suspect. He denied it, of course. I wanted to believe him—needed to believe him. My mother didn't. To pay for the necklace, she confiscated my work-study check until I moved out, and changed my address.

Marcus did eventually admit to stealing the necklace—thirty years later. We had a daughter together, been married, and divorced. He served twenty-six years in prison for a crime did not commit. Once he was exonerated, we briefly attempted to reconcile. I had a dream about the necklace, which caused me to ask him about it. To my surprise, he admitted to stealing it!

"You know why I took it!", he said.

I said, "No, I don't. Why?"

"Because I'm a thief." *Just like that!?*

"You're a thief, okay."

He said, "I was a thief."

As much as I appreciated his honesty, I was dumbfounded! He made no apologies and didn't even offer to pay me back. Granted, it would have merely been a gesture of remorse, but he clearly had none. My mother was right about Marcus.

## Early Belief

I started reading the Bible on Crane Street, more out of my love and intrigue for reading. Reading was learning, and that book on the living room coffee table was big and captured my attention, for no other reason. Marcus presented the Bible in a fashion of control and authority, but dominance and power aren't necessarily negative things. It's about who has the authority and what they believe, that is at the core of the issue.

The Bible starts in Genesis with God creating and giving. In the New Testament again, He begins with giving, so please tell me when He came to take from us! We gave away what He gave us; we refuse to honor His love-ship over our lives. Yes, I said love-ship, not lordship! Father God is always giving to us.

Curiosity led me to read the Bible, and that led me to accept Jesus Christ as my personal Lord and Savior, changing my life eternally! The day I received Jesus Christ as my Savior, there was an immediate difference I experienced. My urge to relax with a joint wasn't relaxation anymore: it was a soft conviction. I knew from the scriptures that my body was the temple of the Holy Spirit (1Corinthians 3:16).

This change brought a sense of peace, joy, and freedom. No one told me once you receive Jesus Christ as Savior, your mind and body experienced a transformation. It was more "Receive Jesus Christ so that you won't go to hell." Salvation was presented as fire insurance, not a love thing!

It was as if I knew, deep within, everything was going to work out well for me. I experienced this hope before it was confirmed by Romans 8:28: "And we know that all things work together for good them that love God, to them who are called according to His purpose."

Although I was not aware of this scripture, it was a part of God's promise to me. When I received Jesus Christ as my Lord and Savior, I received all His words in my spirit, but my mind needed to play catch-up. It was a liking to being born into a family; as a baby, your mind doesn't know the words and phrases of your parents, yet you wholly belong to them, and they belong to you. I belonged to Father God, and he belonged to me because I accepted Jesus Christ, His son, as my Lord and Savior.

I'm sure Marcus did not expect our Bible discussions would cause me to seek God for myself, but I am so glad God led me to Him. I did not know our conversations would lead to seeking Jesus, who changed everything about me.

## Fire on Crane Street

One night, towards the end of 1978, two Molotov cocktails were thrown into the house: one through the living room window to block escape by the front door; the other through the kitchen window to prevent us from using the back door. Fortunately, there was a back porch on the second floor that we were able to use for escape that night. The rumor was Pearl had made enemies with some people in the neighborhood, but we never learned anything for certain.

Through all the chaos, I forgot to grab my birds from my room. "My birds!", I cried. I was heartbroken! My father, who had spent the night, tried to stop her, but my mother went back into the house and rescued them. With the fire station just down the street, the response was almost immediate. After the fire department left, my mother called my grandmother.

I know she was distressed from the house fire, but it wasn't long into that conversation I heard my mother pleading and crying. I had witnessed my mother talk to my grandmother throughout the years that ended with her crying. Although I couldn't hear what she was saying, the pleading in her voice led me to believe my grandmother didn't want us to come there, but she eventually relented.

We left Crane Street, never to return, and moved in with my grandmother, who was now a widow. Before long, one of my uncles felt it was best if she didn't live with us kids, so he bought her another house. He was right. Unlike my uncles and other respected adults, my grandmother's presence did not check my mother's behavior. When you consider Callie Mae Whitmore as her mentor, it makes sense.

## Time to Leave

One evening when my grandmother went to sleep, I don't remember what I did, but it set my mother off. She started with her usual "I never wanted you and your father put a hole in the rubber." This time, being eighteen, I knew she couldn't take me to the youth home and have me locked up.

I said, "What do you want to do with me? Kill me? I'm so tired of hearing you say that to me." She stopped talking to me, but I knew it was time to go! I left that night, more for fear of what my mother might do to me for speaking to her like that. The fear was always in the back of my mind that she would hurt me again, worse than the first time. I called my father, and he allowed me to come stay with him.

My father lived on Detroit's westside on Clifton Street with his father. Both were alcoholics. I was anxious about the change, but I was more scared to stay with my mother. The house on Clifton provided a sense of relief. My father wasn't a bad guy; he was just weak. Whether he was that way because of alcohol or a deeper issue, that weakness ruled him.

The first night, he showed me the bus route and how to get to Martin Luther King Junior-Senior High School on the eastside. I was determined to finish high school. Graduation was just a few months away. Having to catch two buses instead of one took longer to get to school, but the peace was worth it. I wasn't afraid my father or grandfather would hurt me, despite their drinking. They argued when they got drunk, but the arguing never involved me and they weren't violent, so I didn't care. I concentrated on graduating from high school and applying for financial aid for college.

I had room in the attic. When my grandmother left, no one took on the responsibility of cleaning. The house was a mess. The bathroom? I don't think it had been cleaned since Grandma Gertrude left. The bathroom was a dingy pink with matching fixtures: tub, toilet, and pestle-style sink. It took days of cleaning before I felt comfortable using it. The kitchen was small and filthy, but I ate at school mostly.

Without the watchful eye of my mother, I got closer to Marcus. At the time, I didn't know Marcus had been in Wayne County lock-up on numerous occasions for petty crimes, like pickpocketing and purse snatching. It should've revealed his true nature, but in that vulnerable state, I was looking for comfort. All my birds died after the fire. I needed a friend and Marcus was all I had, but he was just as broken and troubled as I was.

I graduated in June 1978. There was no prom, no class ring, or senior pictures. A picture in the back of the yearbook was all I could afford. I didn't feel I was missing out on much. Pictures, prom, and class rings were celebratory things. Sure, graduating from school was a cause for celebration but it was enough to be out of Patricia Mills' house. What I wanted and needed was direction not, the temporary trappings of high school graduation.

I thought of going into the military. I thought I might leave and never come back, but my father said no. Perhaps my father knew my intentions, nevertheless, I trusted his opinion about the military. He enlisted in the Air Force twice: first, after high school, and again when he married my mother. It never seemed to be anything he looked back on with any fondness.

I won a scholarship at Wayne County Community College and chose to study law enforcement administration, thinking it was a people-serving business. My thirty-year career at the Wayne County Sheriff Department taught me law enforcement is not service, but politics. Politics is about helping the very few ambitious.

One night I made the mistake of staying out all night with Marcus. I didn't think my father would notice or care. When I got back, my father had called my mother. I didn't understand my parents' relationship; they talked almost every day. They never divorced, and they never did anything together. There was certainly no concerted effort in parenting, so when he called her, I wasn't immediately alarmed. I wasn't her responsibility anymore. She'd repeatedly expressed she didn't want me, didn't love me. Why would she be concerned with anything I did?!

She must have broken every traffic law in Michigan to get from the east to the westside as fast as she did! She pulled up in a blue Chevy my grandmother gave her, razed hell! I was holding a bag of matching zodiac t-shirts Marcus and I bought from the mall. She tried to rip the bag from my hand, knocking me off balance, and sent my head crashing through the glass window of the front foyer door. Blood streaming down my face, I was stunned. I let go of the bag. She was gone in the same tempest that she came.

My father said and did nothing. My grandfather did the same. It was as if they were afraid of her: she had no gun or other weapon, just a spirit of rage. I understood why Marcus did nothing. It wasn't his family or his problem. But the two I was born to did nothing to intervene or protect me. My father's inaction to the circumstances he created, added to my sense of distrust and loneliness. I wondered, did either of these people (my mother or father) love me? Neither provided guidance. Maybe they couldn't. Was I expecting too much from my parents?

I started at Wayne Community College. My days were difficult: loneliness was my daily companion. Most nights I was hungry, but I wasn't going to steal or do anything to jeopardize my future. To say I was having a difficult time was an understatement, but I knew all these things were temporary and better times were in front of me.

Shortly after the incident at my father's house, I moved in with Marcus and his family. Mrs. Wilson, Marcus' mother, was a sweet witty lady. Her sweet demeanor and heavy southern accent summoned my attention when she spoke. She would tell me, "You're a good gurl. You need to find someone who will love you." She repeated that saying more times than I could remember, along with the statement of "Marcus is no good." That was most times followed up with, "Marcus is my son, and I love him, but I don't like him."

Although she couldn't write or read, she figured out a way to leave her abusive husband and took her three youngest children with her. That took courage, I admired that about her. One of her daughters became addicted to heroin and eventually lost custody of her children and making Mrs. Wilson the primary caregiving of her grandchildren.

There were a couple of other addicts that lived in the house. Anyone who has ever lived with addicts has noticed things have a tendency to grow legs. One of her daughters only showed up around the first of the month to steal. With all the stealing, there was surprisingly, very little fighting. Marcus would have a fit when he didn't get his way, but I grew up in a house of emotional outbursts, so it was more like a pouting to me. Even when Marcus dumped a trash can on his mother, I was so desensitized to abuse, I could not see the warnings.

It was as if stealing from each other was a standard form of treatment. When Marcus' sister Nellie needed a blouse to go out one night, she just took mine. It was a blouse that my mother made me. That night she got shot in the arm. Surprisingly, she managed to get the blood out and there were no holes in it, but I couldn't wear it anymore. It felt different: something about the idea of the blood, and violence stained the shirt differently. I didn't want to wear it anymore, regardless of sentiment.

I didn't understand all the things I thought were bizarre about Marcus's family were in him. He never expressed his opinion about the drug use or the stealing. My love and affection for him led me to compromise my self-worth. I thought with time, Marcus would change. Not that I could fix him, but that I thought we were working together, and eventually he would see the benefit to what I was doing and want the same. The change would occur naturally. We could create a world apart from where we started, but he wanted what he had.

It was a different kind of poverty, if there is such a thing. I grew up knowing we didn't have much, but our house was clean. We each had chores, assigned days to wash dishes and take care of other aspects of the house. The hot soapy water irritated my hands but that didn't exempt me from participating in the upkeep of the home: mother bought rubber gloves for me.

We always had toilet tissue in the bathroom. We ate from plates and drank out of cups; they were melamine, a durable plastic. I'm sure it was a cost-saving thing for my mother with four children, but it laid a standard that I thought was a household norm. We didn't steal from each other, and my mother didn't allow us to bring home items we didn't purchase.

When I became a mother, I understood the rule also protected children against child molesters. I didn't want my daughters stealing but I also didn't want people I didn't know giving them gifts without my knowledge. Child molesters often groomed children for abuse by giving them affection and gifts. Any unfamiliar toys had to been accounted for.

My home environment influenced my idea of cleanliness, just as Marcus lived out his home environment. We viewed life through a different lens; I didn't think that was a problem, but we also didn't value relationship the same things, and that was a problem. With youthful enthusiasm, I thought we made our realities, not our parents or family backgrounds.

What I didn't understand was how influence worked. My naivety wanted to believe Marcus felt as I did. I realized we thought differently, but I didn't think the difference was necessarily bad. I didn't know that God's word said not to be unequally partnered. We had different motivations and desires. We didn't want or value the same things; that was becoming increasingly evident!

Initially, I thought we got along well because we didn't quarrel. I thought that meant we had something special: something we could build a life upon. We didn't argue because I had no opinion about anything: our families, why he wasn't finishing school, what his goals were. We never talked about the stuff that mattered. I understand now that a relationship without conflict is without growth. Both parties are comfortable with the status quo or at least one person is willing to compromise their needs to accommodate the other. This is not love. It is the fear of losing the illusion of love.

Marcus recited scripture not because he believed it, but for behavior modification. He spoke of the Bible as an authority, but out of context. Submission, as he defined it, meant obedience, but they are not the same. Submission is an attitude, and obedience is a physical response to a request made. I can be obedient without being submissive. Nevertheless, all he was looking for was a physical response.

The Bible had a specific place in the house where I grew up, but it just occupied a space. My mother never read the Bible out loud, and we never had Bible study as a family. She would speak of God like he was some faraway entity that had betrayed her. God was standing by while all kinds of awful things happened to her and did nothing. She never spoke of God with love or compassion, but always as an authority.

When Marcus spoke of the Bible, it felt familiar. Even though that familiarity was incorrect, and it violated the grace I heard of years before from Kenneth Hagin Sr. and Derek Prince. I heard more of the inaccurate about the word of God than the correct. As much as I listened to the incorrect, it began to sound right, but wrong at the same time. I didn't know to repeatedly hear the same thing builds consciousness for what you're hearing. The Bible says faith comes by hearing and hearing by the word of God (Romans 10:17).

I wanted to believe Marcus believed in the God of the Bible since he grew up in a church where his father was a deacon. I thought growing up in a church meant you knew the Bible and who God was. I learned neither of these was necessarily true. The Bible possessed a special place in my heart that was difficult to articulate in the face of all these conflicting thoughts and ideas.

I didn't understand then God made man with a void that can only be satisfied by fellowship with Christ Jesus. The Lord Jesus Christ is the only man to fill the God-shaped void in man. All things in Heaven and that are on earth, visible and invisible, whether thrones or dominions or principality or powers. All things were created through Him and for Him (Colossians 1:16).

## Pregnant and Homeless

I got pregnant at 18. All I knew was I didn't want to have my baby growing up in chaos: the chaos of his people or mine. Although they weren't physically fighting, it was unsanitary. The sink was always full of dishes, which brought gnats. The bathroom toilet was ever in need of repair, and there was never any toilet tissue. The floors were forever dirty, and there were roaches, lots of roaches!

I always viewed my situation or condition as temporary. I seldom felt a sense of hopelessness, although my pregnancy provoked me to consider my life more seriously.

I kept the room that I shared with Marcus clean, but the roaches were invasive. They got in my alarm clock, and I put the clock in a plastic bag and hung it out the window before going to school, hoping the freezing temperature would kill them. As soon as I plugged in the alarm clock, I could see them come to life again, now I was genuinely disgusted! It was freezing outside; how did these things survive?

When I lived on Crane, our next-door neighbors had roaches. When my mother saw one roach, she would go berserk and call an exterminator the next day for one bug because one visible roach meant several hidden. Our neighbors didn't seem to mind sharing their house with them. They never called the exterminator, nor did I ever witness them even bother to kill them.

Having a baby prompted me to make decisions for the temporary good, one step closer to a better place. Every interim decision brought its own learning experience, some I appreciated, and some not so much. During these times, I didn't acknowledge the Lord Jesus Christ daily, as I ought, because I was so involved with trying to solve my problems as if I could. The beauty of the Lord is he never leaves us nor forsake us (Hebrews 13:5). Once we are His, we are His forever; nothing can cancel our family position. It's all based on the finished works of Jesus Christ at the cross.

Pregnant and homeless brought their own set of issues. I was scared, alone, and had no support. I had very few options. I couldn't have my baby at my father's. Two alcoholics constantly fighting was no place to raise a baby. Prayed, I didn't have to have my baby there! Marcus' family was a group of people under the same roof who shared the same last name, but I could have a baby in those unsanitary conditions.

Marcus maintained a position of lazing and wallowing in the excuse of "They don't like me because I'm dark-skinned." Every job he acquired always ended for the same reason. I convinced myself into entertaining the fact that he might be right. I suggested going to school or taking up a trade. That resulted in a new excuse: "I don't have no clothes, "to which I responded neither do I! Marcus was busy proving himself an unfit mate, but my eyes couldn't see from all the chaos and confusion of the situation. I wanted to believe he loved me, and that that love was enough to modify his heart to provide for us. That never happened.

The more I attended church and studied the Bible, the more the idea of God's purpose arose. In the beginning, God created man and put him in the garden to tend and keep it (Genesis 2:15). This tells me, man was assigned a task by God. Man's job description continues in Genesis 2:19. Out of the ground, the Lord God formed every beast of the field and every bird of the air and brought them to Adam to see what he would name them. Whatever Adam called each living creature, that was its name.

God gave the man a job and a mental mindset to fill his job description. The tending and keeping of the garden and naming the animals took imagination, so humanity was with a creative ability like God. God spoke, and it was so. I understood my development depended on my relationship with Him. I needed to know God and the Lord Jesus Christ intimately. As a new Christian, I thought all churches taught the same things, but I was wrong!

Marcus didn't care to attend church. He'd rather hang out and gamble: always having money to lose, seldom having any to give. He wasn't interested in looking for a job or going to school to develop a trade. In no fashion was he able or willing to step up to provide for his family.

The more I attended church, the less submissive I became. My default setting to understand wasn't getting me very far in this situation. The more I learned, the less I comprehend. He said he grew up in the church, but he had no interest in attending church. I was confused.

I frequently told Marcus he needed time accountability. It wasn't good, especially being a black man to be hanging out in the hood, shooting dice all day. The only future in idleness was trouble, but my warnings fell on deaf ears. Ultimately, his aimless lifestyle left him without an alibi when he was accused of the crime that stole twenty-six years of his life.

My mother's place seemed the best option: imagine that! It was clean, and there was very little chaos, by comparison to the two other options. The place I was desperately trying to get away from seemed the best way for my baby. But my mother wasn't talking to me and wouldn't take my calls.

Eventually, allowed me to visit. It was during one of my visits my sister told me she was pregnant, but I didn't reveal I was too. I, too, was pregnant. I attempted to get a feel to see if I would be able to return to her house for the baby's sake.

Unbeknownst to me, my mother was still receiving welfare benefits for me. When I went to the welfare department to get medical assistance for prenatal care, they informed me I was already receiving benefits. I remember thinking this lady (my mother) was collecting money and food stamps for me, but I can't get a meal! Like, man, this is crazy! I wasn't going to make a fuss. All this was temporary: my living with her, needing assistance. If I made the government money an issue, she would've denied me the chance to stay there. My mother eventually allowed me to come back to stay with her. I promised her I would only be there until after I had the baby. I didn't share my living arrangement perils. This non-communication thing was the norm in my family.

In the meantime, Marcus got himself locked up again. I wrote every day and visited, as often as I could. I didn't want him to feel like he was alone. Once he got out, he told me, "You didn't need to write every day," and I asked him why he didn't tell me that then. I think he was being mean, looking for a response, which he would do from time to time, but now the relationship wasn't about him and me anymore, we had a child. We needed to grow up.

The stamp was around fifteen cents, plus the time I spent to let him know he wasn't alone. I thought it might encourage him. Whether this was an act out of meanness to watch my response, I don't know. It hurt my feelings, simply because he didn't appreciate my expressions.

Nevertheless, he didn't appreciate those daily letters and didn't mind letting me know it. His moment of frankness caused me to question myself. How much of what I do is for me but benefits others? The five months in the Detroit House of Correction came and went, and he quickly found his way back to doing what he wanted to do, nothing! Soon my hopefulness was replaced by the reality: The man was doing what he wanted to do: absolutely nothing. I was going to be with him, I was going to have to accept that! What an insane thought: taking care of me, him, and the baby. I wasn't going to do that.

Although Marcus wasn't there when our daughter was born, he was serving time at the Detroit House of Correction: for threatening his brother with a gun. With the pocket-picking charge, he got probation. The new offense got him locked up for five months, in those five months, our daughter was born.

I would write every day, visit, as often as I could. I didn't want him to feel like he was alone. Once he got out, he told me, "You didn't need to write every day," and I asked him, "Why didn't you tell me that then?" I think he was being mean and looking for a response, which he would do from time to time, but now the relationship wasn't about him and me anymore, we had a child. We needed to grow up.

The stamp was around fifteen cents, plus the time I spent to let him know he wasn't alone, and he was on my mind, I thought that meant something. And now he says, "I didn't need you to write me every day." Whether this was an act out of meanness to watch my response, I don't know. It hurt my feelings, simply because he didn't appreciate my expressions. But the writing served a two-fold purpose; I thought: for him to be encouraged in that awful place and express my thoughts of love and emotions.

Nevertheless, he didn't appreciate those daily letters and didn't mind letting me know it. Moments of his frankness brought me to question myself. How much of what I do is for me but benefits others? Now the five months in the Detroit House of Correction came and went, and he quickly found his way back to doing what he wanted to do, nothing!

## The Foolishness of Wishful Thinking

One evening we spent the night over his father's. Marcus and I were downstairs in the living room area talking. We didn't have a crib, so she was sleeping in a dresser drawer upstairs in one of the bedrooms. When I looked in the living room window, I saw the reflection of a fire in the room my daughter was sleeping! We ran upstairs and saw the drawer was on fire! An ashtray was left on the dresser, close to the drawer. An ember must have landed in the make-shift bed and caught fire.

Her diaper was a bit singed but thankfully she was unharmed. I was so grateful worried as well. I needed a place to live that was my own. My mother's house was a place of fighting and confusion. It was clean, but the chaos brought its loathing! I hated being there; it wasn't safe there either. I found a place and I started the application process, but I didn't have the security deposit. I called Aunt Audrey and she sent me the money. Praise Jesus for the grace of God!

My ignorance, naivety, or stupidity had limits. When he came home after being in jail, our daughter was about six months old, and that was just the beginning of him being absent from our lives. I rationalized a lot in those days: like him going to jail for stealing because that's what it was. Later he told me the details: on a crowded bus, he took a wallet from a lady's purse. His reason was he needed money, I thought why not get a job man!

I had repeated epiphanies about Marcus. Maybe he thought I was stupid. Whatever it was, it was that thinking that led to verbal and physical fights. Not only was he refusing to take responsibility and care for our daughter while I was at school, once he took her over to his father's house—the house where she almost died!

Why did I believe I could have a future with him? He was a thief and had no desire to be anything else. With all the issues of housing and money, Marcus never tried to help. Emotionally torn, he was my only companion: imagine that my only friend was no help at all. I appreciated his company, but I needed him to help with his daughter.

My hopefulness was foolish because it lacked any substance, only wishful thinking. The studio apartment at 2227 Holcomb Street wasn't great, but it was one step closer to a better place. We were safe, but the roaches were terrible! I was concerned because I was told they would crawl into the ears or nose of babies. I used lots of roach spray in the kitchen and bathroom, but it did little for the infestation.

The reality that I was going to have to raise my daughter alone cause me to start resenting him; I didn't have her by myself! The notion that I would not financially support my daughter was inconceivable; she was a victim. Marcus wasn't a victim. Along with the rest of his behavior: refusing to maintain employment or keep our daughter safe while I was at school, which forced me to go to my mother for help.

That started a new issue of paying my mother for childcare, but I had no choice! I wasn't getting much money between the work-study grant and welfare stipend. Every time I got money, she got money. Was I afraid she might hurt my daughter? Yes, the thought crossed my mind, but again, I needed to trust someone! I was reluctant, but she was also taking care of my niece. I wanted to believe she wasn't that same person that burned me.

I still didn't want to give up on Marcus on our relationship. I tried to encourage him to get a grant to attend Wayne County

Community College with me. He refused, giving the excuse, "What am I going to wear?" *What are you going to wear? Are you serious?* Our difference in thinking lost its attraction.

## Prophesy or Wisdom

I told Marcus, if he didn't get a job, go to school or do something productive with his life, he was going to end up in jail. His response was, "You burning bread on me," an expression of wishing evil on someone. I told him that's not so; it was commonsense. I told him, "Idleness never profitably served anyone."

# The Fall of 1982

After twenty-six years, he was exonerated and won a large settlement from the City of Detroit. He used it to smoke crack and wasted his opportunity at freedom and success. He brought our daughter a nice car and spent the rest on court-ordered rehabilitation programs to stay out of jail. In hindsight, it was good he was taken out of my life. I question whether his intentions were ever admirable toward me. I was carried away by the idea of belonging to someone, desperate for love.

In the fall of 1982, there was a home invasion and sexual assault in Indian Village, Detroit's prestigious historic neighborhood. An unknown man broke into the home of a young teacher while she was home with her infant son. Leaving the boy downstairs, he beat and raped the woman numerous times for hours. The woman described her attacker as a young black man with braids. Her attacker never concealed his face and at no point did she ever mention that the assailant had a cut on his top lip. The man was also described as clean-shaven.

She was given a mugshot book to look at and several men as possible assailants. One of the men she picked was Marcus. The first time Marcus was taken in and questioned concerning the crime, he had a full mustache and a very distinct scar on his lip from a child-hood scrap. The investigating officer questioned him and released him. That officer went on vacation and another officer rearrested him. Before we knew it, Marcus was on trial for burglary and rape! The clean-shaven attacker couldn't have grown a hang nail, let alone a mustache, in the time it took the Detroit Police Department to lock up an innocent man.

Through a later investigation conducted by the Innocence Project, it was revealed that the victim could not identify her attacker in a lineup, which included Marcus and seven other men. The detectives put together another lineup. The only man included in both lineups was Marcus. When the victim still failed to identify her attacker. The detectives suggested that one of the men from the previous lineup was in the present one. With that bit of manipulation, she chose Marcus from the lineup.

I knew he didn't commit the crime because he was with me at the time, but given our relationship, I wasn't considered a reliable witness. The prosecution argued my motives were selfish. The jury didn't believe my testimony. Marcus was convicted and received 20–40 years in prison. It was devastating!

I couldn't believe what happened. Sure, the appeal process had yet to begin, but this meant years of waiting. For what? For him to get out and continue what he was doing before? Regardless of our differences, no one deserves to have their freedom ripped away from them and then dumped by their woman. I felt a sense of duty to stand by Marcus.

When I saw the prosecutor after the case was over, I asked him, "Do you believe he did this." The prosecutor said on the front steps of the Frank Murphy Hall of Justice Courthouse, "It's about clearing cases. If someone goes to prison that's innocent, hopefully, they will get out on appeal." He followed that by saying, "You're going to school for law enforcement, right! You should know some of this stuff." *Sending innocent people to jail is just about clearing cases?* I read no book that substantiated that type of injustice or procedure.

I fasted and prayed for seven days. I needed understanding and I believed real discernment came from God not from forming your interpretation. I sensed this was much bigger than what I was looking at. The Bible says lean, not to my understanding (*Proverbs 3:5*). Deliverance comes from feeding on the Word of God, not by man's interpretation of the circumstances. I knew God didn't do this, but He could fix it!

During my fast, I received an inward witness of peace that exoneration would come for Marcus and some other realities, many of which I couldn't articulate with words, but sensed spiritually. The turnaround was coming! After three days of fasting, I was no longer hungry, and my mind was very sharp. My prayer time was focused; it was phenomenal, a natural high.

When I reached a point of peace during this fast, I ceased fasting. God didn't tell me when or how he would be released, but I knew he would be. That was my first time fasting and praying for a specific thing. Being a baby Christian, I felt I needed to quiet my flesh. I wasn't sure how to treat the information I was receiving during this consecration.

The progression of days brought peace in the situation: a knowing that Marcus was going to be exonerated. He, Father God, didn't tell me to wait for him. I thought it was the right thing to do. I didn't ask Father God for his wisdom; my sense of devotion was ruling my common sense. My understanding of loyalty was all wishing thinking. I was in the infancy of my walk with Father God.

I called the woman that accused Marcus of rape. I got her number from the court transcripts. I was surprised she spoke with me. She didn't seem upset by my calling her, which I thought was strange. I expected to be hung up on, but instead, she told me, rather calmly to get over him. "Somebody raped me," was her response. Not, "He raped me." I remember thinking, she wasn't sure who raped her. I felt sorry for her, but it wasn't Marcus that committed that terrible act.

After hanging up, I thought about what she said about getting over him, and that "somebody" raped her. For sure, some black man raped this white woman and some black man paid. I also feared my boldness in calling her. I never called her again.

The prosecutor and the accuser surprised me with their complacent behavior. Deep within, I sensed Marcus and I weren't going to share a future. Not so much because of the conviction, we were two different kinds of people. I needed security and for our daughter to be safe; he could care less about where or how he lived. The situation presented a sobering reality. Regardless of the depth of my love and affection for him; I knew we were too different.

Our value systems weren't remotely close: I valued education and having a work ethic. He wasn't going to keep a job and had plenty of excuses. My mother could see my pain during this devastation, but she didn't voice her disdain for Marcus. Instead, she said, "I believe he'll get out, but maybe this is what you needed to get away from him!" I received her comments with no response since deep within, I agreed with her.

In the wake of the conviction, I pushed our differences aside to give him a support system. I felt that's what I would need under the present circumstances. Again, these were my thoughts, not God's direction. I soon learned I was just a tool to use for whatever he thought he needed or wanted. He knew I was very sympathetic and caring. He misused me until I got a revelation and said enough!

I honestly was trying to support him and wait for him. When the abuse over the phone started, that made an impossible situation intolerable and downright insane. I excused the verbal abuse for a couple of years because I couldn't honestly say I wouldn't feel or act as he did. Considering our relationship when the wrongful conviction came, he didn't deserve unconditional devotion and commitment. But I still wrestled with my emotions. To support him seemed only humane.

In hindsight, the whole situation was a question of self-worth: the woman that gave birth to me thought I shouldn't be here, and her husband was unavailable due to his sickness. I never heard the words I love you growing up from anyone in my family: not my parents, aunts, uncles, or grandparents. Did I believe they cared about me? Yes, I did, but they never said so. These were my examples.

I lacked any concept of what love looked or felt like: it was a foreign idea. I honestly didn't know how to value myself. Sure, I had salvation, and I attended church (wasn't going to hell), but no lessons were highlighting my worth in Christ Jesus. No sermons enforced the idea of as Jesus is, so are you in this world (1 John 4:17). That boldness that came from valuing myself in Christ Jesus, manifested later. Not a worth based on the ownership of earthly things or the accolades of men but based on the price God spent: the blood of Jesus shed for me!

## My Journey into Motherhood

The birth of my daughter impacted my thinking differently. This little life that came from this union. My life was a result of my decisions, but it wasn't just my life anymore. It was my daughter's future. I had no clue how to raise a child. It wasn't like I had any examples, so I turned to God, the Bible, and the church.

Finding a church was an adventure all by itself since all churches didn't teach the same things. Some don't teach rightly dividing the word of God and introduce it in the proper context. All the Bible is God speaking, but not all for me. The new covenant is for me.

I met an older guy at school, and he invited me to his church. New Breed Christian Center I attended their church for many years. Pastor Harris taught the Bible. His style of teaching held my attention. The older gentleman was always kind to my daughter and me, making sure we attended church every Sunday by bus until I got a car. He loved the Lord Jesus Christ and only spoke to me about scriptural things.

One morning, as we were waiting on the bus to go to church, we observed a man jogging. He said to me, pointing at the jogger, "That is what the world does for health, but we go to church and hear the word of God for health." He knew about Marcus, and when the wrongful conviction came, he didn't take advantage of me in that vulnerable state. Instead, he prayed for me. When my daughter needed shoes, and I couldn't buy them, he brought them. He was always a gentleman; he was God's grace during that time.

## Wake-Up Call

I will dive into my time at Wayne County Sheriff Department soon but since we're on the subject of Marcus and our time together was coming to an end, it makes sense to talk about a realization that struck me one day at work.

I was observing inmates in a ward area called the day room. I was working in the same type of environment Marcus was now living under sentence. On one day, I overheard a conversation with some inmates playing cards. One guy says to the other, "I'm getting ready to call this bitch to send me some money." He picks up the telephone, appears to be talking to someone in a loud voice coupled with profanity, then slams down the receiver.

He comes back, high-fives another inmate, says something to the effect of "screw that bitch" and went back to playing cards. A few minutes later, he got up and made another call. Whether he was talking to someone or putting on a show, I received a lesson that day.

I had a wake-up call; that was me on the other end of that phone. How many times, over three years, had Marcus hang up on me mid-conversation because I wouldn't send money or buy a television for the second or third time. He would call me back a few minutes later, and like an imbecile, I would accept the charges, paying for my mistreatment.

At that moment, I decided I wasn't going to be locked up with him anymore. I accepted his cruel behavior as just a response to the stress of being imprisoned for a crime he didn't commit. My patience had faded from the abuse I experienced. That day marked a turning point: I filed for divorce, stopped visiting, stopped accepting phone calls. I took my life back.

I wrote him a letter stating my new position and why. Tolerating that kind of treatment by someone who claims to love you is only acceptable when you don't value yourself. I was yet to come to know in the eyes of Father God that I had tremendous value in the sight of God. I was done being treated terribly and paying for it. Love doesn't hurt, it gives.

Unless God has called you to jail ministry, visiting jails and prisons is a stagnant world. There is a strong possibility you are being used or misused depending on the person's character. The world of incarceration is an environment of predators. Now, if it's your family member, this may not be applicable, depending on the relationship and character of your relative. When a person is under sentence, they will tell you whatever they have to, in order to get what they want or need, be it a visit, money, or whatever. The question is this, is this God's best for you? The answer to that question must be no! Jesus Christ died for you; Jesus Christ is God's best!

Conversations ceased with Marcus and our daughter when she stole her classmate's-colored pencils. She waited till her classmates left the classroom, then she went through the desk drawers. The theft wasn't the only part of this situation: it was the forethought she put into concealing the matter, that spoke volumes. It was the thinking that needed to be corrected. Most actions, positive or negative, have a meditated thought process at work. The planning was my most significant concern.

I told him about the incident, and he thought it was funny. Whenever he called and spoke with her on the phone, I would listen to the other end. I needed to know what he was saying. She told him what she did, and his response was laughter. His laughter spoke of approval for her; she laughed too. Our daughter knew her father was in jail for a crime he didn't commit, and we believed God would deliver him, I kept no secrets away from my daughter.

Before the conversation ended, I spoke to Marcus without our daughter on the phone. As much as I didn't want to, I decided no more phone calls. I explained to Marcus my concern about negative influence and the impact of approving of destructive behavior from her father. I don't think he realized the importance a father holds in his child's life.

Little girls love their fathers: whether good or bad. He's the first man in their lives: he's the first date, the first boyfriend, and the primary leader. He's the example. He lays the foundation for the future man in her life. I was not sure if that was the best thing to do, but I needed to protect my daughter. His position as her father wasn't to support non-productive behavior. Perhaps, he couldn't be supportive as a father, and I wasn't going to change his mind or give him another perspective.

## The Innocence Project

The Innocence Project was established in 1983 to address the injustices occurring in the criminal justice system. In the mid-'90s, my mother called me and said an organization contacted her regarding Marcus and they were trying to reach me. I met with an attorney from The Innocence Project at a restaurant in downtown Royal Oak.

At this point, he had been under sentence for at least sixteen years. Although we were no longer in contact, I still wanted the best for him. I still believe he would be released. This organization was the answer to my prayers. In 2008, The Innocence Project succeeded in getting Marcus released from prison.

## ❧ CHAPTER 8 ❧

# *Searching*

## For Family

Accepting Jesus Christ as my Lord and Savior meant being born into the family of God, it was more than a religious act for Hellfire insurance, but a family.

There was one problem: I had no parallels of family to draw understanding from. Perhaps I was experiencing family in all those houses: my father and grandfather's, the Wilson's, and back to my mother's, where all families had different dynamics. This sense of family played out in my mind as a group of people pressed to live together by circumstances, void of meaning, or purpose. Is that what family was? I hope not!

Salvation meant not going to Hell, not that I was being born again into a new family. It was love that Jesus came, and it was love that Jesus died for me. A sacrifice I couldn't see in the family dynamics I had previously lived in.

I was born into a family: my father (albeit absent), my mother, and my siblings made up the dynamics of my household. Better or worse, my siblings and I learned how to treat and value each other from this environment of family. The verbal abuse, rants of rejection, the threats of abandonment, and mental manipulation created a behavior code—not necessarily a right or practical standard—nevertheless, a form we took with us in one way or another when we left our mother's house.

Since love was more of an idea than a reality, how do I adjust to this new love reality? I knew how to retreat from rage and rejection, but Father God didn't have fits of rage, nor was He absent, He is ever-present (Psalm 46:1)—that was a foreign concept. The salvation of Jesus Christ offered a family idea I found difficult to grasp.

The God-shaped void inside me was yearning to be connected to Father God and be loved. But with naivety and ignorance, I allowed a fleshly man to stand in that position—Marcus. Not intentionally, but I allowed him to distract me from the fullness of Jesus Christ. God existed long before I was born, and I sensed I existed for something bigger than what I could see or understand.

The first churches I attended after receiving Jesus Christ as Lord didn't elucidate the fact that Christianity is about family or that I was a new creation in Christ Jesus, something that never existed before. Therefore, if any man is in Christ, he is a new creature old thing have passed away, and that all things had become new (2 Corinthians 5:17). The decision to accept Jesus as my Lord and Savior reconciled me to God through Christ Jesus (2 Corinthians 5:18). This reconciliation of Christ was God working to reconcile the world to himself, not imputing their trespasses to them, and has committed to us the word of reconciliation (2 Corinthians 5:19).

Most churches reminded me of the Ten Commandments, which is impossible to keep. The Ten Commandments were given to the children of Israel to bring them to the end of themselves. Paul said, in 2 Corinthians 3:7 it is the ministry of death written and engraved on stones. Ten Commandments were given to the children of Israel, not the church.

I attended church after church trying to find someplace to grow in the things of God and raise my daughter. I went to a word-based, non-denominational church at the invitation of a friend. I joined and was a member for over twenty years. I learned the Word, but very little about rightly dividing scripture. I knew church structure by attending and serving. There was no warm family vibe; it was a business; sometimes it felt like my workplace. I thought that was the way it was supposed to be.

# For God

Not being one to make New Year's resolutions in 2002, I endeavored to know more of God. Kenneth Hagin Sr. was the first man to talk to me about Father God. I heard him say plenty of times, "God and his word are one John 1:1." His voice was so calming and persuading, my desire to get to know God and his ways meant I needed to make listening and studying God's word, from the beginning to the end, a priority.

I needed more than the weekly sermons I was getting. It wasn't providing me with the person of God and Jesus Christ. I was shopping at Best Buy when I saw the NIV translation of the Bible on CD. Then I went to Border's and found an NIV version of the Bible. The plan was to listen and read the Bible at the same time to charge my mind with the Word of God. Reading and hearing used different portions of the brain. I wanted to inundate my soul with the Word of God.

The process took an entire year. During that time, God became a person, not just a faraway divine entity waiting for me to mess up to punish me, but a real person, up-close and personal. As I was standing at the kitchen sink one afternoon, washing dishes and praising God for all the many blessings He had recently given me, I heard loud and clear, "You don't love your children more." I was the only one in the house. I knew this was God speaking to me. I was hurt at that moment because he was correct, of course. Then I heard the tithe. Till this point, I wasn't a consistent tither. As a single parent, I reasoned when I needed things for my children, I would use my tithe when I ran short. I had put my children before God and my trust in the county, not God.

The tithe belongs to God, and it is a privilege to give. I don't have to tithe, it's a relationship thing. God loves me whether I tithe or not, just as he loved Israel. God loved Israel, and they were just like me, happy when things went well and unhappy when things didn't go as they would like, and when they complained, but God loved them anyway. His love didn't change for their complaining. Until the Ten Commandments were issued, and even then, God told them to build an altar (Exodus 20:24). Although God gave them the Ten Commandments, he still gave them away to honor him: the offerings on the altar system.

When God became a person, my thoughts about him changed. I wanted to please Him, not just attend church but attend church to learn my Father's will and ways, to fellowship, and to serve. My serving was unto my Father God and the Lord Jesus Christ. There is joy in serving; it wasn't a church duty; it was a family thing.

My church didn't highlight Jesus Christ: His finished works at the cross, scourging on the way to the cross, and what all that meant. Most sermons missed the essential ingredient in bringing us together with Jesus Christ.

## For Wisdom

I thought understanding would give me freedom from repeating my parents' mistakes, but only the Lord Jesus Christ can and will deliver you from past tragedies, flaws, or mishaps. Only God can change our past, present, and future!

The local bookstore's self-help aisle became my hangout spot, whether it was Borders, B. Dalton, or Barnes & Noble, they all offered a plethora of literature to give a sense of a better you. Although, after a while, all self-help books began to sound the same, no spiritual revelation, no real way to apply the information received from those books. I reached a point of emotional exhaustion with the feel-good-about-yourself self-help books; there was no deliverance.

The journey of redemption and freedom came when I read a series of books called Spiritual Warfare, Hereditary Traits, and The Living World. Those books, along with the Bible, woke me to my family's mental condition and mine. I needed to understand a basic biblical principle: demons had entered my life through abusive activity. They must have a legal right or a gateway of opportunity. No one can put a curse on you unless there is an opening. Those books ended with prayers; however, none gave Jesus Christ his place in spiritual warfare.

As the bird by wandering, as the swallow by flying, so the curse causeless shall not come (Proverbs 26:2).

## CHAPTER 9

# Wayne County: My Beginning in Law Enforcement

I attended Wayne County Community College, pursuing a degree in Criminal Justice and Law Enforcement Administration for two and a half years, taking time out to have my daughter. One of my professors told me I wasn't law enforcement material, I didn't listen. Thirty-plus years later, I wished I would've listened and asked more questions.

After graduation, I applied for several departments, one of which I got hired. In November of 1984, I applied to the Wayne County Sheriff Office as an uncertified officer (who knew there was such a thing). The position came with excellent benefits. But low wages. My grandmother told me it was a good job. Since she retired from the county, I valued her opinion. Nevertheless, like all opinions, it's relative to the present time.

I attended the police academy in 1987; my eyes began to open to the kind of people I was working with and how I was supposed to treat inmates. The police academy influenced me into a way of thinking. I realized my professor was correct in his assessment of my personality and character, but now I was in too deep! Fear ruled my mind.

How was I supposed to treat inmates? The police academy provided fundamental criminal law and defense tactics. As a recruit, part of my requirement was to keep a notebook for review by the sergeants. Plenty of notetaking, which is essential for report writing, but still no people serving skills emulated. Being a police officer wasn't a people-serving business at all.

My academy classes centered on performance; competition for number one in class was a recruit's preoccupation. Being number one had its perks; it got you noticed. Getting positive attention could mean a specialty or discretionary job in the future. The state of Michigan mandated all the training. No training for the interrelation portion of the occupation, but there was an unwritten rule that we deputies were better than the criminals.

I felt like we're all just people in different uniforms in different roles. I soon learned deputies weren't better or smarter, just blessed not to be on the other side. There is only one decision between the deputy and the inmate. Over the years, I observe that one decision could cause those around you to view you as an inmate of sorts. As if you become someone else by one mistake, just as there is only one decision between the believer and unbeliever: that decision is a hell or heaven choice, a devil or Jesus' choice.

The career and environment woke me to the understanding I was in the wrong place. I had invested time and energy, a degree in Law Enforcement Administration, and now I was academy trained. There were a few things I wasn't going to do at this point. My daughter would've been the person that suffered the most for the decision to change my career direction. I wasn't going to short-change my daughter by doing something else to generate an income, taking more time from her.

The county kept its promises in my grandmother's time to give medical at retirement and a pension. The public servant has lost the benefit of medical at retirement through economic changes and politics. The politician gets medical, but not the worker.

The possibility of promotion existed in the county. With certification came promotional opportunities and getting out of the jails. I knew it was just a matter of little time before opportunities presented themselves. That would allow me to do something different. I got several offers after starting at the county.

The Michigan State Police was just one of them. The home interviewer, a female trooper, followed my brother around and told me, "Your brother's driving with a suspended license." I thought, how am I supposed to know that? That should've been a clue what I was giving my life to. She interviewed every member of my family.

At the end of the interviewing process, she told me I needed to divorce my incarcerated husband. I explained he was innocent. She said, "That might be true, but the two environments don't go together." I refused to divorce him at that time, and the Michigan State Troopers declined my application. I felt like a job shouldn't harness that type of control over my life. Little did I understand, the county would do the same thing! I wanted to make a difference; I wanted my life to stand for something; I didn't understand I needed to pray. God knew what he made me for and where I should be.

This same corruption that incarcerated Marcus for twenty-six years for a crime he didn't commit was the same system that brutalized and intimidated the men and women in the uniform. In November of 1984, I joined the Wayne County Sheriff's office. In 1985 the internal affairs unit conducted a sting where they recruited a juvenile inmate to solicit some floor security officers to bring in cocaine for him. They used a deputy at the time that worked on road patrol. That road patrol officer brought in McDonald's bags containing narcotics.

The jail administrators gave Sgt. Kent Booth permission to operate the sting for ten days. In the end, five deputies were arrested for delivering narcotics to the jail. The juvenile trustee received a sentence reduction for compensation. The event of arresting the deputies was so fantastic. Sgt. Booth, along with a few of his companions, entered the roll-call room asked a few deputies to come forward, read them their Miranda rights, handcuffed them, and led them out the roll-call room only to them in a holding cell, where everybody could see them.

The Michigan Supreme Court threw out the case for entrapment in 1990. In hindsight, I should've left then, but I still didn't want to believe it was that bad. So young, so dumb, so optimistic! While I was working at the county, I got involved with Sam, another officer in my department. He was fun to be around, but we had no business being together.

The marriage was best described as a flash in the pan, but I got another beautiful daughter out of it. It was over about as fast as it started. We were both young, but I believe it was my insecurities that were the primary issue. I felt unrest in my life that magnified our differences. The things that were funny when we met grew to be mean. My insecurities seem to rest all over the place, but I didn't want my daughters to be casualties of my bad decisions. This relationship was like the environment, the people I worked with weren't my friends, but we spent so much time together, it gave the illusion that we were.

CHAPTER 10

# A Single Mother

I didn't enjoy being a single parent; it had a lot of challenges. I passed up opportunities for promotions because promotions meant a shift change. Unless you were part of the clique (which I wasn't), chances are it would mean an afternoon shift.

As a single parent, my life wasn't my own. I had to limit my daughters' exposure. I was the first line of protection for my daughters. The best way to protect them was to shield them from my work environment. Dating wasn't an option. I couldn't risk giving my phone number to the wrong guy (this was pre-cell phone days).

For years, I would go to concerts by myself or with my daughters. We all enjoyed jazz and when Pat Metheny Group came to the Detroit, we developed a habit of going. I was the number one role model (not perfect but wanted them to have an idea). I took them to church, and frequently prayed over them as they slept. I prayed for myself to give them a better childhood than I had.

I tried to work a straight day shift with weekends and holidays off for my children to experience a sense of normalcy. When I couldn't, I asked my neighbor across the street to watch my daughters. With ten years between my daughters, unfortunately, my oldest daughter turned into a babysitter for her little sister some weekends, so I could make extra money. Sometimes I took them to my mother's house in Detroit.

My daughters asked me to stop working the weekends because they told me, "Momma, we would rather have you at home on the weekends than to have more stuff and go places." Since they both felt I needed to be at home, I stopped the weekend overtime, and a fantastic thing happened, God supplied. We still went out after church on Sundays, and we never missed a meal. I prepared meals at least three to four times a week because I didn't like them eating fast food, but Friday was pizza night.

When my daughters became adults, I took the sergeant exam and got promoted. Close to retirement, I felt the change offered the opportunity to do something new and give me supervisory experience. I was praying what to do next after the sheriff's office.

Knowing Jesus Christ died for me and what all that meant wasn't my consciousness at the beginning of my walk with God. Going to the church provided me with a sense of keeping the law. Consequently, I felt condemned, because the law doesn't save man. The more condemned I felt, the more mistakes I made.

I didn't know there was no condemnation to them that are in Christ Jesus (Romans 8:1). I didn't know how much God loves me, nor how Jesus Christ paid the cost for my sin at the cross and how the finished works at the cross that made me righteous, in Christ Jesus or that righteousness is a gift from God and God doesn't take back his gifts (Romans 11:29).

Spiritually exhausted is what I was. All my seeking only led to a sense of works and working to make myself right, none of which is the truth. Attending church gave me and my daughters a routine, not a revelation of the love of God. Whether this was good for them, I wanted to believe so.

They knew the name Jesus Christ, the nucleus of the Bible. With all my intense reading and studying of God's word, I still missed one essential character of God, which is love. God's love is permanent; it's unchanging; it has taken years to wrap my mind and heart around the idea; my relationship with Father God is lifelong. It's not my good deeds; my righteousness is in Christ Jesus. That was a new kind of love. Where I came from, it was an unbelievable idea!

# Wayne County: My Life in Jail

In 1988, the jail came under court order to provide humane living conditions for the inmates. After non-compliance for fifteen years, the Wayne County Circuit Court appointed the Wayne County Executive as the receiver of the jails, removing the sheriff's control. The court order created jobs to promote compliance: titles they now call directors and deputy chiefs. This court order provided an environment that was humane for the inmates and deputies because the officers spend 8 to 16 hours a day in the jails. The order cited categories to be corrected: visitation, inmate recreation, mail, clothing and linen sanitation, discipline and grievance process, maximum security, health care, food service, training, law library, classification, staffing, population limits and overcrowding. Under the court order, inmate care was a priority.

It became a safer environment for the officers, since the mandate included staffing. There was little overtime during those days, and all the floors were open in all faculties. By 2019, the jails had fallen back into their original inhumane conditions. Inmate health care and food service were privatized. The psych inmates did not receive prescribed medication to due cost-cutting. The psych inmate housing reeked of feces and urine.

On any given weekend, there are no nurses in the jails to provide inmate care. For medical codes that required hospital runs, there was no staffing to accommodate emergencies. As a sergeant, part of your duties is floor security rounds, meaning entering the inmate housing area. For that few seconds of entering the ward, you are at the mercy of the inmates and with no deputies to respond to a code 10 (officer distress code). I stop working overtime on the weekends because I feared for my life.

Toilet paper, soap, and c-folds (hand drying towels) were scarcely available. Imagine trying to explain that to an angry inmate that only believes the deputies are lying to him! Bringing your own toilet paper and hygiene products became necessary tools for survival. Then there was the lack of rubber gloves, a universal precaution. Officers resorted to purchasing rubber gloves. Law library and recreation were a thing of the past because of staffing issues.

The filth took its toll on the officers as well as the inmates. Having to live and work in unsanitary conditions affects your mental and emotional health.

Cleanliness and supplies are scarce unless the Department of Justice showed up to inspect the jails. For those few days, there were cleaning supplies and equipment are readily available. When they left, so did all the cleaning supplies, equipment, and rubber gloves till they returned.

When the DOJ showed up, the leadership came to roll-call and talked to the deputies with dignity, as if they cared. Perhaps for those few days, it's a reality that the troops run the jails. When the DOJ left, so did the value of every jail personnel from the commander to floor security officer, along with everything that makes working in the jail humane.

## ❧ CHAPTER 12 ❦

# *Sam*

Sam and I worked together and became friends. We should have stayed friends. The relationship lasted for little more than five years. He would come to visit, he would bring a gift for my daughter, this little gesture meant so much. I thought he was a caring and thoughtful guy.

Robert was the type of man whose momma was first and foremost, and she ruled his thinking. The kindness shown in the beginning was a phase. His father and mother raised him; his father worked at an auto plant while his mother was a homemaker. It seemed like an ideal situation. At the beginning of our relationship, his parents separated, which led to their divorce.

There was a breakdown in the marriage. The respect between them was gone, they spoke to each other with such cruelty, and they didn't care who heard it. Robert sided with his mother during the separation, although his father told him to stay out of it. Robert would call his mother daily. The conversation started with "How are the kids?", referring to his siblings. He didn't view himself as their sibling, but more of their elder.

My church attendance had diminished to a non-existent state. So, when the marriage proposal came, I figured "Well, he's working." We were already living together, so why not? There was a little church around the corner from the apartment. I went to the pastor's wife to talk about this marriage business but couldn't get an appointment. After a few attempts, I gave up the idea of seeking guidance before getting married a second time.

Living together before marriage cursed the covenant. Intentions to marry isn't enough to justify or fix the brokenness created by cheapening the sanctity of the nuptials. Robert had pornographic material throughout the apartment, hidden in various locations. I found a VHS cassette tape in the basement, on top of a vent, during a work-out session. What I didn't know was how serious porn addiction was.

Honestly, I didn't know or understand there was such a thing as an addiction to watching people have sex. I didn't understand the spiritual implications of living together outside marriage; I was told it was wrong but never told why. Sin opens the door to judgment: that's sin payday. I worked full time, cooked, and cleaned: the apartment, washed clothes. We split the bills and some other living costs like food and toiletries. We were roommates with benefits.

His money was his, and mine was mine. God designed marriage; it's a blood covenant. When a woman moves in with a man void of a ceremonial commitment, she cheapens herself. He gets all the comforts of marriage with no commitment. No wonder when problems occurred, because problems will occur, he wholly detached from the situation. There was no significant event to put this man on notice things had changed.

Marriage is for the woman, and if he loves her, he will marry her. The ceremony wakes up the man to his responsibilities. Living together before marriage is frequently an unconscious lifestyle adopted because it seems financially advantageous.

The pornography affected his affection toward me, albeit unintentionally: this activity opened the door for Satan to operate in the household. He was, by comparison, a better guy than Marcus. He had a job, at least. This comparison should've happened since it was all based on a natural way of thinking. Marriage shouldn't take place on the comparison of better or worse. We moved in together, got married, had a baby, and split the bills. Robert brought cars and electronics. That's when I realized him having a job means nothing if he's not responsible. He was a kid at heart; his mother approved of everything he did. This momma's boy was ready to take care of himself and himself alone.

## The Mother-Son Relationship

My mother-in-law and my husband were very closed, as a mother and son should be. But the influence of her position and her way of thinking infiltrated my husband's method of viewing the marriage, none of which was in a positive light. My husband's best friend was his mother. They talked on the phone every day sometimes several times, like two girlfriends!

The hate and disdain my mother-in-law had for her husband nurtured the hate Same had for his father. I couldn't compete with my mother-in-law for my husband's attention. Consequently, when we began to experience challenges in the marriage, talking to him about our finances and lack of affection, I got stonewalled with comments like, "I ain't having any problems." Essentially saying, "If it's a problem, it's your problem." I guess I wouldn't have a problem either if I had a roommate keeping the place clean and when I didn't pay a bill, she paid it! So engrossed in my ineptness, I became a frequent visitor at Border's self-help, self-improvement, and psychology sections.

Again! I made a series of unwise decisions that landed me into single parenthood. I needed understanding, so I thought! My self-improvement attempts were only making matters worse. It was all secular, worldly wisdom that offered a step program that didn't work, leaving me feeling like a failure. I was getting to understand with no application. Self-help, self-improvement, and psychology books can't give heart transformation, you can only get from the Lord Jesus Christ.

## The Turn of Events Brought Me to a Church Home

I don't believe I was actively seeking love when I attracted Sam, but a weakness in me him. That weakness, by God's grace, was going to be arrested in my generation. True love is only experienced and found in the relationship with God and the Lord Jesus Christ. While this second marriage was disintegrating, a friend invited me to her church on Detroit's Eastside.

The energy of that church moved me to want to join; the pastor spoke with authority and conviction. I lived forty-five minutes away. The task seemed daunting: two kids, forty-five-minute drive every Sunday! I remember feeling like this is where I belong, but forty-five minutes every Sunday with my kids, I told the Lord, "I needed some help" to pull that off.

Monday through Friday was work before I went to work, getting two people together for school. In hindsight, the church decision was a soul decision, a heaven and hell decision, therefore an eternal conclusion. I didn't know how much God loved me and wanted the best for me; it's difficult to trust what you don't know. But God's unmerited favor was flowing in my life. His grace is sufficient.

In the summer of 1995, the apartment complex I was living in announced a rate increase on rent, which was to take effect at the end of the lease. That summer, I committed myself and my daughters to move, where? Wasn't sure yet? But I wasn't going to pay double the rent when I could buy a house.

To pull it off, I worked overtime every day. My daughters stayed at my mother's since it was summer. I was practically living at the jail. That summer, I paid off my jeep, saved money for a house, and by September, I was house hunting. I went to Barnes & Noble to buy books on house buying and financing.

The process was intense. I had no experience with buying a house, how to obtain financing or what to look for during walk-throughs. I prayed to be at the right location. I made Hebrews 11 my chapter for meditation. The very first house I looked at, I bought, but not right away. I wasn't sure if it was emotions or my realtor's voice ringing in my ears; he kept repeating the address. We looked at several other houses in the same neighborhood. Then we returned to the first house he showed me. I realized my realtor was right! I made an offer.

My daughters and I moved in October, right before the apartment lease expired. Father God heard and answered my prayers. The church relocated around the same time I bought my first home. It was within a two-mile radius, making my church attendance regular. The proximity of the church from the house removed the struggle. Father God worked it out when I forgot about it!

I continued reading the self-help material when all I needed was to read the Bible and meditate on the scriptures. The Bible has promises backed by the throne of God and the blood of Jesus Christ.

Our differences showed themselves when our assignments changed. I got a position where I would be off weekends. This change diminished our time together; his complaining seemed to make sense at work, considering the work environment, but that was who he was. The complaining about older drivers wasn't funny anymore; it was mean. In addition, he wouldn't attend church with the girls and me.

## The Problem Wasn't Psychological It Was Spiritual

I might have read almost every book by Nathaniel Branden. The Psychology of Self-Esteem, this text caused me to examine myself through the science of psychology. Reading books on self-esteem intellectualized my inefficiency in loving and appreciating myself. Which only led me to buy more books, causing me to rely on my ability. Every book gave me a greater sense of independence from God, which isn't God's best. God's best is dependence on Him to bring you to His purpose.

From my childhood, my consciousness took shape by my surroundings. That environment gave me a sense of awareness that became my consciousness or self-awareness for functioning in that setting. God's word says in Proverbs 22:6, "Train up a child in the way he should go: and when he old, he will not depart from it." The amplified version of Proverbs 22:6 says, "Train up a child in the way he should go (and in keeping with his gift or bent), and when he is old, he will not depart from it." God made all of creation with a special gift and calling. Satan hates God and has been attacking that from the beginning with Adam and Eve, Cain and Abel (Genesis 4:2). It seems Satan hates women intensively; it was through a woman Jesus Christ came (Matthew 1:18).

The woman was the vessel of God's choice to deliver the savior to the world. I am sure that made her a number #1 target for Satan. She serves as matriarch of the family; her role is vital. The position of a woman, being a female, is incredible. We are a powerhouse fashioned by God, at the beginning (Gen. 2:20, 23) to serve in an invaluable position, and a helper for God's man, Adam, who I like to add had a job and a relationship with God (Gen. 2:15–17, 20).

Now for all the good, God made woman got twisted when she yielded to Lucifer's suggestions (Gen. 3:1–6). One thing I love about God's word is when I meditate; imagination takes over. This back-and-forth conversation Eve had with Satan makes me wonder. How long did this dialogue last? Was it hours, days, months, years, it's not clear? And where was her husband, Adam? Right there, scriptures say (Gen. 3:6) when this exchange was happening. When she eats, was he there, or did she take the fruit to him at another location? No, scripture says she took the fruit and ate it. She also gave it to her husband with her. Now, this doesn't elaborate on whether it's a physical together or a spiritual together. For whatever or however it happened, the woman was created for man's good but was deceived by Satan. The man followed the woman, instead of the creator of the woman, God.

A friend of mine would say, "The man is the head, but the woman is the neck that turns the head. The head isn't going anywhere the neck won't let it go," I would laugh, but I've learned there's a ring of truth in it. As women, we set the tone in our families; we are wives, mothers, sisters, and daughters. We are domestic support, homemakers. We are the first person the baby comes to know; we are the primary teachers; this is the most relevant job a woman will ever have.

Being a mother is the only job that will make a difference a hundred years from now. Because what we teach our children or don't teach them will be in the future. Therefore, God states in his word to teach a child in the way he should go. The child becomes an adult, and the adult teaches the child. This is how generations educate. My mother did to me what she learned. My grandfather was

75

abusive, and my grandmother was passive-aggressive; my mother was a product of the two.

The first person I had a relationship with burned me and continued to abuse me verbally by telling me, "The only reason you are here, 'cause your father put a hole in rubber, I never wanted you." That went on until I was eighteen years old. I thought little of myself—that exchange of verbal rants developed many unhealthy habits and thoughts.

This second marriage brought the realization that the way I felt about myself was the primary influencer in my decision-making process. Indeed, my mother couldn't love me, and my father didn't love me. Maybe I am just unlovable, was my core thinking. So, to generate positive self-esteem and self-image, back to the self-help section, I went to find more secular reading material that sounded good, Branden or someone else that caught my attention.

At that time, I didn't understand that I desperately needed a relationship with God, and not man's idea about how I should view myself, based on changing circumstances and the fickleness of people. The constant teasing at school and my mother's rejection left me scrambling for a place to belong.

Alone, as a child, you can't reason why your mother is mean and hateful. All my self-worth came from what I didn't get. Reading books on self-esteem would help me value myself and reflect better decision making. Honoring Yourself by Nathaniel Branden spoke of pride as a positive emotional experience, just as self-esteem is. He described pride as a vice to embrace and virtue to possess; this line of thinking was supposed to give a sense of self-worthiness to honor oneself, placing all my worth and idea of self squarely all about me. Sounds good, but it's unscriptural.

The Bible has a lot to say about pride. None of it is good (Proverbs 16:18). Pride comes before destruction (Proverbs 11:2). When pride comes, shame follows (Proverbs 14:3). In the mouth of the foolish is a rod of pride (Proverbs 29:23). A man's pride shall bring him low: but honor shall uphold the humble in spirit.

The series of books I read by Nathaniel Branden on self-esteem: Breaking Free, Self-Alienation, The Disowned Self, The Psychology of Romantic Love: A New Vision of Man/Woman Relationship, and The Power of Self-Esteem: An Inspiring Look at Our Most Important Psychological Resources. After reading several of these books, I still was missing understanding and a sense of fullness. That sense of fullness was genuine love, not a cosmetic sense of affection. I was on information overload but had no core answers, still running on empty.

I started looking for a church again. I knew the answer was in the Bible, and the church taught the Bible. I wanted Sam to be a part of the church selection process, but he wasn't interested in going to church. From the small church in Taylor, Michigan, to the big church in Detroit that a friend invited me to, none of this saved the marriage; it ended in divorce. My searching was for a way, not The Way, which is Christ Jesus (John 14:6).

Christianity isn't about a systematic way of doing things; it's about family, and since I came from a family where dysfunction was the order of the day, I had no parallel to draw. The year my partner and I divorced, so did his parents. They had been married for over twenty-five years. What led to their divorce? Not sure. It doesn't take twenty-plus years to know you're in a bad marriage, while being cruel to each other.

I filed for divorce because I didn't know what else to do. I was exhausted from trying to talk to someone who didn't want to talk, and repeatedly told me I was the problem. Sam was there, physically, but absent otherwise. I learned from this man you can be present, but unavailable, just as my father was unavailable.

My choices were a reflection. I wanted better for my daughters; I felt like this was an impossible situation! Nothing is impossible with God, though (Matthew 19:26). But before I filed for divorce, I got involved with another guy. A lousy idea, horrible idea! Although it wasn't my plans, it was a friendship that went too far. I entertained his conversations.

Sure, I could blame my husband or all those secular books on self-esteem, but the reality is blame only frees your consciousness of no accountability, no responsibility, and no growth. I was so frustrated with myself! I refuse to be the person cruising through life, never learning from my wrong or uninformed decisions. The countless hours in the self-help/psychology and spiritual sections of bookstores taught little truth, only gave information.

Pornography and masturbation are cheating on your mate, just like sharing intimate details about yourself or your mate with a friend. It opens the door for demons to eradicate your marriage and your life. Satan comes to steal, kill, and destroy (John 10:10). The spirit of masturbation is a demonic force that opens doors to other evil influences.

## Sexual Sins Doorway

I did not know my husband's extracurricular activities were so spiritually deadly, I sensed he was relieving himself through porn and masturbation, but I was too ignorant to understand the repercussions of his actions. As I said before, I didn't know you could have an addiction to watching other people in the act of sex. Sure, there was the frustration it was causing, but I thought, how do I demand my husband to perform? My thinking was you don't, and you can't do that!

It sat in later, the reason he had no desire to perform, and when he did, it was always brief, was because of the pornography. It opened the door to sexual sins (Proverbs 26:2). His inability to perform put me in a vulnerable position, coupled with my ignorance.

I made myself available to a man who would listen to me and pay attention to me. It was ignorant to think I couldn't or wouldn't be with another man. Pride led me to believe I was above that type of activity! The more I talked to Enyi, the more my mind became willing. What the mind entertains, the body will follow!

Sam never asked me where I was going or when I was coming back because he didn't like me asking him where he was going. His response was always, "I'll be right back," never telling me where he was going or when he would return. The situation was a recipe for disaster. I allowed myself to get talked out of my clothes; literally. That was the point of no return for me. The shame was like carrying around an albatross. The marriage was toast.

I would leave the house, wouldn't say anything, take the girls to my mother's house, and be off entertaining myself as if I was single, never lying about where I was or what I was doing. There was no dialogue between us. No accountability as a marriage partner. Did I love him? Did he love me? I believe so.

The counselor helped little for two reasons: my heart was someplace else, and Sam still refuse to take responsibility for anything in the marriage. First was the communication issue; we couldn't talk about anything. Second, was there was no financial or personal accountability. We were like roommates, but that's how we started right! We went to two or three sessions, only to have no more than what we had before, in terms of the quality of a relationship.

I felt like we were both pretending; the lack of communication didn't change. For his part, I didn't feel like he or the marriage was important enough to continue to work at. I didn't need him; he added nothing in terms of the quality of my life. I did most things by myself. I am sure my heart condition played a significant role in counseling being ineffective. My heart was no longer in the marriage.

My friend, Enyi listened to me, and he talked to me. Even with being served divorce papers, the communication didn't change between Sam, and I didn't change. He said, "You are the problem, so you need to leave." That fit right into the casual remarks I would receive from his mother. My mother-in-law offered her unnecessary comments telling me, her son, "Sam is a good man." *Was she kidding?* He wouldn't pay the rent for us when I was off on maternity leave. *A good man? Is she nuts?* A good man would support his family. She also added, "If you ain't careful, you're gonna lose him." I thought, he could go immediately, if not sooner!

## CHAPTER 13

# *Years of Single and Self-Discovery*

I was single for thirteen years. It was odd to me once my divorce took place, and I was alone, why I didn't feel like before. It was like I got a whole new lease on life, and I didn't want a commitment. I didn't know what I was doing, and you can't keep doing the same thing looking for a different result. I think it was Einstein who said that was the definition of insanity. I needed to do something different to get a different result. It was strange once the marriage dissolved also went the longing for intimacy, at least in the natural.

I continued to frequent the self-help/psychology section at the bookstore. I kept in contact with Enyi for a while after the divorce, and he talked of marriage; I knew I couldn't do that, neither did I want to. But I enjoyed his company, and deep within, I knew the time would come to end the relationship.

The day came when he told me he would sell drugs, if necessary, to generate an income, later saying it was a joke. I believed he would sell drugs. I think people joke sometimes as a safe way to tell you the truth. The jesting, as he wanted me to believe, came from his consciousness of chicanery. So, the time came to end the relationship.

## Self Help in One Book: The Bible

Visiting the self-help section at the bookstore became less frequent. I found the truth, the Word of God. I joined a word-based ministry,

80

and I took my daughters to church twice a week. They needed it, and so did I. I read books though just more of Kenneth Hagin Sr. It was from Kenneth Hagin's teaching that I came to understand what the Lordship of Jesus in my life meant. His cassette tape teaching on "right and wrong believing" stayed in my cassette player for over eight months, why? Because my pastor said, it takes at least eight times of hearing something before it becomes a part of your thought process. I needed my way of thinking to be transformed by the word of Christ Jesus.

Kenneth Hagin said in that teaching series: it is the inside man that gives the outside man permission to do what he does. That revelation changed my view of life and the things that I thought were okay. The Lordship of Jesus Christ in my life personalized my walk. Listening to the Bible on compact discs and reading along bears repeating; I needed the word of God deep within me. It was like sitting at the feet of Jesus I sensed His presence as he was telling me the history of creation and the Father's love for me.

That exercise was worth every moment it made God/Jesus Christ/Holy Spirit alive, a real person, and that changed my walk with God. God becoming a person made sin unattractive, I mean seeing him as a person forced me to see Him as someone that my actions or inactions could hurt because he loves me so very much.

The tithe belongs to my Father for kingdom work. I'm experiencing salvation because my spiritual ancestors before me returned the tithe. I believe he is who the Bible says He is. Because God was alive and very real to me by this point, I made it my business to return Father Gods' money. I say return because everything I receive is from the Father, and the tithe is his, not mine!

It's seeing Him that way that made it easier to tithe; it's a part of my relationship with my Father; it's a family thing. I get to tithe, not I have to tithe. It's a love thing; love makes me what to please Him, not a church obligation, but a love privilege.

## Enyi

Enyi was an Igbo Christian man, a friend who encouraged me to see life differently. Often during my career at Wayne County, I would meet someone that took an interest in counseling me about my career choice. My friend Enyi was one of those people that told me I needed to get another job, more fitting for my personality.

Being stubborn, we had many debates about this subject and many others. I couldn't see his point. I thought I was humble in thinking and believing I did not differ from my colleagues. He gave many explanations and illustrations to explain his position. I couldn't see me through his eyes, but I think if I could, I would've valued myself enough to leave the job and leave him alone as well!

## Our Conversations and Debates Lead to Research and Meditation

Enyi and I would debate about, as he put it "African Americans are lazy." This conversation was ordinary between us. A part of me agreed but grew uncomfortable hearing him say, "African Americans were lazy," being one myself. After one of these debates, I went to Borders bookstore; this was the pre-internet boom. I spent some time looking for information about the Igbo culture and particularly the Igbo man. I found two books.

When I read a book, I envisioned having a conversation with the author, so I wrote notes in the margins. I read both books simultaneously. Reading the books prepared me to converse with Enyi on a level that wasn't driven by my emotions. Men wrote both books, and I did that intentionally since I was debating a strong, opinionated Igbo man.

One of the books was titled Anioma: A Social History of the Western Igbo People by Don C. Ohadike. I don't remember the title of the other book; it was something to the effect of identifying an Igbo man in a crowd. It was a skinny pamphlet book, helpful but not as impacting as the book titled the Anioma. Both books he borrowed and never returned. I used the books, not as a matter of fact but just a point in the debate, as both were written by Nigerian men, as I recall.

Anioma spoke of the Portuguese being the first to enslave people from Africa for economic gain some two thousand years before. It further stated the people of Anioma took part in the slave trade and provisioned trades because their homelands had long been integrated into the tradeoff, a region which itself had links with inter-regional, multi-commodity commerce.

This book also spoke of an Aboh woman in 1841 who owned over two hundred slaves whom she kept producing palm oil and yams. In Asaba, Onitsha, and other places, men became slave-owning chiefs almost overnight.

So, my debates with Enyi were that his people owned and sold slaves; they participated in the slave trade and benefited from both sides. It also said during the Atlantic slave trade, the people of Anioma, like many Igbo groups, shunned the prospector slave raiding, even though they engaged in the kidnapping. The business of slave raiding was something Enyi's mother confirmed. His grandfather took part in slave raiding and abduction, killing those that were too young, old, or weak.

The book went on to say that a chief of Aboh recalled the painful side of the end of slavery in the lower Niger by observing, "When the slaves left, their owners wept." Robbed of their slaves and therefore their investments, many owners became as financially challenged as the ordinary citizen. It was the British that ended slavery in West Africa, not the West Africans. It was viewed as a military defeat by many Aniomans. They were appalled by the military failure.

The slave master and their slaves would be equals under the new British law. There was no financial compensation to the slave owners when slavery was abolished. No such provisions could be found in the antislavery regulations to amend owners' rights over other human beings. With the stroke of a pen, colonial administrators dissolved two social classes (slaves and the ruling class of chiefs) and created two workers. Freedom for one, a reality for another!

The more I read and thought about these things, the more I realized that perhaps this man might not know his history. Sure, he knew Nigeria gained its independence in 1960, and he knew little about the Biafran war. But to the degree of the practice of slavery and slave trading, he was ignorant. One evening, Enyi started with a rant about the lazy African Americans, and I asked him "Which is worse, a thief or a lazy man?" I don't remember his answer exactly, but our debates on African Americans being lazy ended that day.

I shared with him about the books I read and how, when America ended slavery, it was still going strong in Nigeria. The Nigerians took part in the kidnapping and the murder of their neighbors. It took another race of people to resolve the atrocities of slavery in Nigeria. I think I did the most talking that day. He sat silently, which was a first for him since his African Americans are lazy phrase came on the heels of additional derogatory remarks of how these people have been here (in the United States) all this time and weren't rich, because according to him, "They are lazy."

That day, I asked him the question several times: "What was worse, the thief or the lazy man?" The lazy man will work. He takes a little longer but gets the job done. A thief works but steals while working. "I think the thief is worse," I told him. We never had that conversation again. But I appreciated the way our debates caused me to seek information for understanding his culture and people. His response was silence and asking to read the books.

If we could see ourselves through the love lens of Father God, we would know our worth. God sees us as worth the blood of Jesus (John 17:7). Jesus said all things you have given me are from you. The blood of Jesus came from the Father; he and the Father are one (John 17:11). In John 17, the prayer of Jesus Christ declares and gives color to us being family, the many times Jesus addressed Father God as "O Father", with such endearment, as Holy Father (John 17:11) and O righteous Father! (John 17:25). Who else could pray the most precious and perfect prayer for the believer but Jesus? In Father God's eyes, we are precious!

No commitment is always fun. The other guy always says he loves you; he doesn't have to live with you; he's doesn't have to work. When the divorce was final, Enyi proposed. As much as I thought I loved him, the reality was: we would never trust each other. Why should we? I didn't care what he said, by this point, the situation was a wreck! This man claimed to be a Christian. Now I knew in this spiritually decayed state of divorce and adultery.

I wasn't fit for any relationship. I pondered it and declined the offer; it wasn't right for either of us. I needed to remain single for a while to focus on understanding myself and the spiritual ramifications of this mess I made. I started reading all kinds of books again! I repented. I felt like that wasn't good enough. I needed to do more to deserve or earn my right place with God, not knowing Jesus Christ bore all my sins at the cross and what that meant.

## Order/Rule versus Compassion

One of the other things we discussed was how I wasn't cut out for law enforcement. I realized Enyi was right. Why? I cared too much for people to be influential in law enforcement, and only by God's grace was I able to retire, after thirty-plus years of service. God created every person with deliberate intent in mind for kingdom work. I was not different of my own volition. I wasn't better or smarter. I didn't keep every oath. I'm different because of the Father God, Jesus Christ, the Son, and The Holy Spirit.

I'm a new creation in Christ Jesus, and Jesus Christ is my righteousness (2 Corinthians 5:17, 21). I didn't understand thirty-five years ago what receiving Jesus Christ as Lord and Savior meant, it meant more than I realized. I was too compassionate to be effective in law enforcement. My thirty years in that career spoke more of God's grace than for my purpose and assignment.

I didn't last that long by design, but by God's grace. God created each person with a purpose and plan for the kingdom; each one of us is fearfully and wonderfully made (*Psalm 139:13*). See, law enforcement is a field designed by the government to enforce laws created to provided order. I used to think all laws came into existence to curb sin; well, that's true and untrue at the same time.

Let me explain. In the beginning, when God created man, there were no laws. It was only a relationship; God would visit the man in the cool of the day (Genesis 3:8). When the Ten Commandments were given generations later in Exodus 20, God knew the man couldn't keep the law. He told him what to do for Him to bless him, what a good God! God made compensation for the man before he sinned because he knew the man couldn't keep the law.

The sacrifices gave man the avenue to experience God's goodness, saving him from the wrath of violating the law. I venture to say God didn't create man to keep rules but for a relationship with Him. Sin entered the picture and modified God's original design. If a man stayed in a relationship with God, he wouldn't need laws. This relationship with God has a modifying quality; it's a love thing! Love won't create an environment where people are destroyed or hurt.

Love edifies; love protects; God's love operates to help people live their best lives. Love is ever ready to believe the best of every person; law enforcement didn't allow me to perform at God's best for my design. I genuinely love people and want to help them. Perhaps I wanted to live the compassion I didn't get as a child. All my debates with Enyi took form in understanding when I retired from the Sheriff's Office.

I realized I was not too fond of the place's system but loved many of my coworkers. The love for my coworkers overshadowed the disdain for the environment and design. Yes, law enforcement is a ministry. It exists to protect and serve the public. The government creates laws to be prescribed by law enforcement officers. This occupation is best for soldiers, types to maintain order where the bureaucracy of an organization doesn't influence their mental capacity. Not for the compassionate type.

## Enyi More Than a Friend

When the second marriage deteriorated from lack of communication, a friend found me, and he listened. It wasn't right, and no amount of reasoning would give rise to making that present situation right, because it wasn't. In my eyes, his opinion lost weight since the relationship shouldn't have been. As short as it was, I felt it could never be between us. Why would I trust him? Would he trust me?

Although I grew up in a home of conflicting emotional events, right and wrong were preached by my mother, as if it was a place of divine order. She was always saying, "two wrongs don't make a right."

I considered myself a child of God, for whatever all that was supposed to mean. At that time, an extramarital affair wasn't somewhere—anywhere I was supposed to be. It violated every idea or belief of what was correct or sound.

To add insult to injury, he claimed to be a Christian also and would recite scripture verbatim by memory. As crazy as it was, I admired that quality about him; I never lost sight of the relationship's inappropriateness. As fate would have it, the relationship ended when I got divorced. The reality was the relationship came to be from dishonesty. Regardless of what my ex did or didn't do.

The environment for another man to become a part of my life was both our faults. My mother's voice would ring in my head: "two wrongs don't make a right." That was the most conflicting six months of my life; I felt like I was going to lose my mind. What this man taught me was always viewed in the light of the relationship. That perspective limited my ability to receive our sharing's fullness since I always felt condemned and judged by the liaison. I repented.

## Information and Revelation

In reading books on spiritual warfare and sharing with a Christian friend I worked with, I learned that pornography was very addictive. He told me God delivered him from the bondage of masturbation, and that's how he lost his first wife. He explained to me it was an uncontrollable urge, but God delivered him from that bondage.

God doesn't force us to do anything. He is the ultimate gentleman! Pornography cheapens the female gender; it makes the woman appear to be always ready, which is unrealistic. God made us beautiful and made us where life passed through us because God is the giver of life, not women. Pornography affects men in how they view women for the negative. It short circuits his ability to express love and affection. Attending church, I learned from my pastor, the number one need for a man in marriage is sex, and for the woman is communication. It takes Jesus to keep that together.

I don't believe there is very much communication happening in pornographic movies; the naked truth, given the material, and its male-centeredness, talking isn't necessary. Sam told me the Playboy magazines started as a teenager; they were in the home; he never said who brought them in the house. The masturbation happened because of the arousal of the pornographic material.

Pornography always portrays a woman as ready in the movies. No foreplay required. In the magazine, she's habitually perfectly beautiful. The man has to do absolutely nothing. What woman can live up to that? And are we supposed to? God never intended for a woman to be misused; she is to man a helpmate (Genesis 2:18).

When the marriage ended, I experienced such condemnation—for the lack of affection and appreciation from my husband and the extramarital affair. Now I was a single parenthood again! Being alone was some place I was familiar with, but this time, I have two responsibilities. My bad, uninformed decisions affected other people's lives, innocent people, my daughters, who didn't ask to be here.

Once the divorce was final, I promised myself to remain single. Not to say that decision was right, but condemnation, guilt, and shame prompted more incorrect choices. I refuse to have men over my daughters. I thought this marriage should've worked. He had a job, and he was fun. My idea about marriage wasn't enough to build a world around. God created marriage. So, God must be in the marriage for it to grow.

We didn't value the same things, and since we didn't appreciate the same things. That reflected in how we treated and viewed each other. We saw credit, money, and intimacy differently, and we couldn't talk about it, it was crazy. Not being able to talk about the core issues made us both vulnerable to demonic activity from masturbation and porn. These vulnerabilities brought other people on screen and off.

My friend, Ann, could see I was torn and struggling emotionally. She was the one that suggested counseling. Another friend suggested different counselor who was useful when they were experiencing difficulties in their marriage. Sam and I went to him with the same results as before. When I went by myself, the primary counselor said, "You need to be all right with what is going on right now in your life," she said. "I'm not trying to help you stay married."

I thought, okay wrong counselor. But was she? I needed to be alright with what was going on. All this was a waste. The marriage failed. My daughters grew up in a single-parent home. I joined the church and took them twice a week. I understood the mess I made. I needed Father God to wash my daughters and me in the water of the word (Ephesians 5:26); change in my life was only coming through Christ Jesus.

In the beginning, Robert said he believed in God, but what does it mean when someone says they believe in God? A belief in God must be defined. Is it Jesus Christ we're talking about or some universal force or some material thing? I didn't have enough development to ask the questions and to assess his response to the inquiry.

Even to ask someone are they saved needs to be defined, salvation is defined differently by different faiths. What local church they belong to are only clues. Only when God says, "yes," are you ready, otherwise you're still not ready! The Godhead has got to be the center of your life: The Father, the Son Jesus Christ, and the Holy Spirit. It would be best if you had them orchestrating in every area of your life.

Every Sunday, the word of God was taught, and my daughters learned the word of God. I could say we weren't equally yoked, but we were both lost and confused. Father God kept me and loved me despite my stupidity. So many things that could've gone wrong that didn't.

## ❧ CHAPTER 14 ❧

# *Wayne County: Endless Overtime*

The officers assigned to the jails work approximately fifty-six hours per week (unless they get FMLA paperwork from their doctor). That may not sound so bad. Travel time is not a part of that time; you got to get to the faculty for roll-call in most cases, for the fifty-six hours to start. The days in the jails are 8.1 hours, 0.1 is roll-call, and roll-call is a mandatory activity. Including commute time, officers devote at least ten hours a day to Wayne County Sheriff's Department.

Overtime is sixteen hours, tack on the two-hour commute. That brings the total work time to eighteen hours, which leaves six hours to shower, sleep, eat, spend time with your family or go to the gym. Okay, no family or gym, but sleep, eat, and shower. The seven to nine hours of sleep recommended by the medical community is impossible for the deputies assigned to the jails.

The jails are understaffed, and the staff is overworked. The effects of this environment are overlooked by management or disregarded. The average deputy is overweight by fifty pounds. A low estimation, I think! Being overweight has its issues: diabetes, high blood pressure, joint problems, risk of heart diseases. Compound that with the county executive instituting a high deductible health care plan to save the county funds, in this high-risk job. Now, going to the doctor costs the county employee more money, in addition to the already high prescription cost.

This cost-saving measure takes place on the backs of the people employed by Wayne County and its retirees. Wayne County has more appointees than Oakland County, a more affluent neighboring county with a more robust economy. At any time, it has 10–14 directors, more than Ford Motor Company (thirteen directors) or Daimler (eight directors). The taxpayers of Wayne County shouldn't have to pay for the mismanagement of nepotism.

While overtime runs out of control at the Sheriff's Office, officers are working additional shifts, hoping to go home after they reach the allotted fifty-six hours. Only to be told by some sergeant the jail needs emergency staffing. They need to work another eight hours. In recent years, the department would order officers that had worked over sixty-four hours. When they refused, they received discipline— for being tired or wanting to spend time with their family. In either case, ordering an overworked deputy doesn't solve the substandard management problem; it creates a morale and discipline issue.

There are only 168 hours in a week, and if you're working over sixty-four, that leaves you less than one hundred hours to tend to your life, sleep, shower, eat or talk to your friends and family, forget about getting exercise and your mental health. When do you clean your house or do laundry? The reality is no amount of money is worth living your life in the workplace.

When you're exhausted from working overtime, you don't have the patience for the people you love the most. When you're stressed, you don't go home and go directly to bed. You lay there wired; it takes longer to wind down. When you're burned out, you can't think straight. Your body is stressed; your digestive system is out of order.

When your sleep-deprived of being overworked, your mood and memory are challenged, your behavior is impulsive. Depression is knocking at the door of your soul because you're exhausted. Fatigue is a slow killer. When you're worn out, you look for ways to relax and mellow-out because you know you need to.

But if you don't know Jesus, your ideas for winding down could kill you, because the world says, "Have a drink." Alcoholism is nearly three times more likely among police officers; police officers suffer addiction 20% to 30% more compared to the general population.

The lifestyle of working sixteen-hour days, sometimes seven days a week, in a negative environment, is damning for your mental health. Sure, two of those seven days may be voluntary, but the negative surrounding is debilitating by itself without the constant forced overtime.

The trap of overtime is you think you need it. You want to buy more things for your family, but in this case, less is more. The more you work, the less you have to give of yourself. The more you labor, the higher your risk of injury. On two separate occasions in 2019, two deputies working a double shift injured themselves at the very last hour of their second shift. The county personnel office refused to pay both of them. The refusal to pay injured employees for sick time off, resulting from an on-duty injury, would seem illegal, but is common practice in the personnel office.

The overtime also serves as a gap for the county to adjust retirement to pay more into your pension and medical. Because the reality is while everything is costing more, the overtime works as a smokescreen. Once that smokescreen is in place, you lose all sense of the things that matter until sickness occurs or make a poor judgment decision resulting in discipline, which may lead to termination. There is no mercy given by the administration to the overworked deputy that makes a mistake.

Additionally, the straight overtime rule, instituted by the Wayne County Executive, to save money. Five years ago, the Wayne County Executive negotiated all county employee contracts with the penalty clause of hours worked don't include benefit time received. You only receive benefit time for coming to work eighteen days in a month. If you take a day off after working sixteen hours, your overtime is at a straight time rate: no time and a half.

Is it saving? Yes. Was it the only way? No. After this saving clause took place, the executive office found some millions. Hiring is a constant process, along with the low wages you pay more for medical and pension. It takes three years to become vested in the pension plan system, leaving before those three years means Wayne County keeps your money. Why would I want to fight with this apparatus that works on discipline and overtime? Wayne County systematically steals from its employees, one way or another.

Thirty years ago, people took government jobs for the benefits and health care insurance at retirement. Medical is gone when you retire, and you pay for it, along with a stipend. Your pension is reduced and taxed. The overtime worked during your career as part of your final compensation, that's no more, now it's based on your salary at retirement.

## Modern-Day Bondage

Where you start isn't where you finish. In my situation, I honestly thought law enforcement was a people-serving career. I was wrong; it's politics 101. I didn't go into this field to get paid well, but to make a positive difference. I was warned at my home interview by Cpl. Pace that there is a lot of overtime. I thought, "Good I could take care of my daughter." Her Stride Rites were expensive, and I was purchasing them every six months. Thank God for layaway because otherwise, I don't know what I would do about school clothes. The idea of overtime meant my daughter would have everything she needed from this point onward. Little did I know the overtime was going to be my life!

Sure, materialism is a part of our culture's fabric, but this is more than materialism. Where I started wasn't where I finished. The more overtime I worked, the more emotionally exhausted I became. I started on the afternoon shift (3:00p–11:00p), but the afternoon shift wouldn't allow time with my daughter. I went to midnights, thinking I would have more time with my daughter, which turned into a nightmare.

On midnights, I was introduced to ordered overtime. FMLA didn't exist in 1985; I got ordered daily. On one occasion, I went to shift command and told the sergeant I couldn't stay because I was too sleepy. He asked me if I was refusing an order. I said no, went back to my duty station and went to sleep.

No sergeant made rounds that day. I think they knew it was terrible, but they could do nothing about the overtime situation.

The overtime was so abundant, a management decision was made to place floor security officers on twelve-hour shifts. Twelve-hour shifts were terrible, but I could put my daughter to bed. The twelve-hour change lasted about six months. I then went to days, because that's what my daughter wanted. I didn't want to get up that early, but I did.

My focal point was my daughters; they kept me from drowning in county politics, policies, rules, and poor management. The rules and policies caused division among the officers. Observing the rules and never getting write-ups gave you the illusion that you were doing better than everyone else.

Throughout my career, a common thought was we needed more blacks and women in command. That wasn't true. More black people in charge didn't create racial equality, and neither did more women in the ranks create gender equality. It provided an appearance of fairness. As a black female sergeant, I observed the female sergeants, both black and white, fighting to prove they could do the job. I never felt I needed to be a man to reach work performance equality. I would jokingly say to my partners, "like this is the first time you ever been somebody," meaning you become somebody because of the uniform or the stripes.

It seemed like the uniform, and the position gave substance to some that they would otherwise not have. Overzealous to enforce policies at all costs, like that policy violation, is so disruptive in an environment where the very reason it exists isn't managed correctly.

## Relentless Discipline

The overtime in the jails throughout my thirty years has always been there. However, under the leadership of Sheriff Napoleon, overtime ran out of control. The faculties are mostly staffed on the weekends by overtime. Now add discipline to an already stressed group of people, and what you have is a mentally, emotionally, and physically exhausted staff the department takes advantage of any given day.

What do I mean by any given day? When some deputy chief or chief makes rounds in the jails, that's nasty! Why? Because there are no cleaning supplies. That always results in a plethora of write-ups for command staff and deputies.

As a commanding officer, you serve an officer a write-up for leaving his station door open to go to the restroom. Perhaps that officer is sleep-deprived and didn't remember. Maybe they thought they shut the door. I've been that deputy that worked sixteen hours yesterday and the day before, and the days start running together. Have you ever been so tried you see things out of the corner of your eyes that aren't there? Well, I have.

The write-up may sound justified if you don't know the housing setup of the jail floor design. On the jail floors, the security measures are stringent. When a deputy leaves his station door unsecured, there are still two doors between the inmates accessing freedom to a hallway. There would be another door before accessing the elevator that would enable them to leave the floor.

An inmate can't access the elevators without having an elevator key and getting past two deputies to get on an elevator. On any floor that the elevator would stop on, there would be another deputy. So, leaving a door unsecured is essential, but the sleep-deprived deputy that has been working three doubles in a row needs rest. Giving this officer a write-up is saying it's your fault the jails are inadequately staffed. Still, putting things in writing always bore future consequences at the sheriff's department; the discipline process is relentless.

The above circumstances of an inmate walking off a ward to freedom have never happened in the thirty-plus years of working for the sheriff's office. Every inmate escaped that occurred where an inmate escaped from the floor, involved an inmate being misidentified by them switching their armbands, plastic bands with distorted pictures were the biggest threat to prison escape in a world of predators.

## Write That Man Up

"Write that man up." Words I grew to hate. The last time I heard those words, a deputy who consistently worked sixteen-hours shifts, left the building between shifts. A lieutenant asked me, "Did you give that officer permission to leave the building?" When I said no, it was followed by "Write that man up." This corporal left the building to get something out of his car and returned to receive a write-up since he failed to get permission. He left for less than thirty minutes. This lieutenant had a reputation of issuing reprimands for any reason, which made my options few. Write the corporal up for failing to notify me or take a write-up for refusing to write him up.

Later during the shift, this same lieutenant asked me, "Are you going to serve that write-up?" I stated, "Yes." He repeated the "yes" with such delight, I was surprised to hear so much joy over something so trivial. He quickly rose from his chair and said, "That's not what it looks like." I said nothing, because why engage in the apparent oppression of a man for no good reason.

Undue stress is what I saw, this corporal gets is a write-up for leaving the building for a moment when he spends all day every day at work. I was not too fond of this kind of write-up because the very person telling me to write them up could do it themselves, but rank allowed them to direct the sergeant to do it. There are times a write-up is warranted and provides a layer of corrective action, but not every time.

A corporal is asleep in one of the closets because he volunteers for overtime every day. "Write that man up." You've warned him numerous times, but he can't seem to help himself. It seems like a twofold issue; why would the county allow anyone to work like this, and why would he do and he's clearly exhausted? Disciplining this guy seems like a complicated way to correct his behavior. Why not put a cap on how much overtime people can work? This corporal, I was ordered for write-up so many times I grew fatigued at the mention of his name.

One day, I had to write him up twice for the same offense: sleeping. He was asleep in a closet on an unoccupied floor. Then he was asleep by the gym while he was supposed to be observing the inmates playing. Sometimes he would leave the building to nap in his car. He would take too many inmates to the law library: having more inmates than chairs to accommodate them. This corporal led me to explain to my lieutenant that I was uncomfortable writing him up for events I didn't witness because I thought something was wrong with him mentally. I didn't want to call the man crazy, but he had some adjustment issues, if from nothing more than a lack of sleep.

I realized taking this position with my lieutenant could have gotten me a write-up since the essence of what I was doing was refusing an order, I had a level of inhibition in dealing with this corporal. He had a gun, and he obviously couldn't realize he needed to go home and rest.

The administration makes up policies for everything that serves them. A procedure to cap overtime wouldn't suit them because it would restrain them in ordering officers to work double shifts. A system of that nature would require caring about its employees, which Wayne County does not.

Discipline is progressive, meaning for every infraction, the penalty becomes stiffer till you reach termination. Wayne County will essentially allow a person to work themselves to death and discipline them all along the way.

## Separated to Control

People in this environment separate themselves by rank, race, gender, and often levels of discipline. This separation is an illusion to give themselves a position of authority. However delusional or self-absorbed it may be, it just prides the primary form of self-righteousness.

They are completely neglecting the fact that we all are working for the same entity and subject to the same rotten treatment. Sometimes being white might curb consequences that someone black may experience. Am I saying the sheriff's office is racist? What is racism anyway, according to Wikipedia, racism is the belief that one race is superior to another. It may also include prejudice, discrimination, or antagonism directed against other people because they are of a different race or ethnicity, or the belief that members of different races and nationalities should receive inconsistent treatment. Based on this definition, I guess I'm saying the sheriff's office practice racism!

For thirty years, I watched this practice unfold. For example, a few deputies can be involved in an incident all sworn by the sheriff and certified by the state of Michigan, but two are black and one white. They all initially have their police powers removed: removal of police powers is the inability to identify yourself as a police officer and carry a firearm under that authority. It's at the sheriff's discretion.

Under the administration of Sheriff Napoleon, police powers are moved for a tip. With little to no investigation, running to a code in the performance of your duties or your significant other calls the sheriff's office and tells someone you stole toilet paper. Neither of these incidents is a gun-related incident. The process of discipline is a tedious one at the sheriff's office.

First, you're relieved of your police powers; then, you're removed from your work assignment, depending mostly on the severity of the alleged offense and skin color. Typically, there is no penalty or light-duty assignments, but the central station in Jail Division One is close to a light duty assignment. It's a glass box located on every floor; it's called a central station because it's centrally located in on the floor, in front of the elevators.

Management has used this as a limbo of sorts, where they may put a deputy and keep them there for eighteen months or longer. The best part about this assignment is the minimum duty and responsibility. The not-so-good part about this assignment is you're a spectacle for everyone to see. Whenever I saw a deputy assigned to the central station, I thought only God knows the truth about the circumstances. My prayer for them was one for mercy and God's grace because the department was merciless.

The awareness of discipline happening unjustly and unwarranted contributes significantly to workplace morale being at an all-time low. It would not be easy to believe all this was happening under the leadership of a black sheriff. Most weeks he's out of town (or so we're told). With predominately black appointees, he leaves the operation in the hands of the undersheriff, a man who has a disdain for people of color and particularly women.

It's an illusion to think, black leadership means black equality. His skin color doesn't determine the sinful nature; it determined by his belief system. Things aren't done blatantly at the sheriff's office, so it would seem being black and a female, my sense of awareness would be sensitively tuned to these matters. For every situation that black deputies fall victim to penalties, the effects are long-lasting: no police powers.

It seems small, consider all the training endured to achieve certification by the state. Without police powers, there is no lateral movement, and there are no opportunities for promotion. It is an endless punishment for the rest of your career. It shouldn't be easy for someone to take what you have earned without a legitimate reason. Sure, there are times police powers should be confiscated. Gun-related incidents and domestic disputes fit in a high-risk category for suspension of police powers. Having police powers is a serious responsibility and not to be taken lightly.

## Politics Makes Strange Bedfellows

When I was hired by the sheriff's office in 1984, taking police powers wasn't commonplace; it was almost unheard of. It meant something to be a deputy sheriff; the public and administration respected you. You were a part of an elite team. You never heard of scandal about the sheriff's department.

The ranks (commander, captain, lieutenant, and sergeant) once served as a form to provide structure. Those holding the positions now would be well advised to remember it's an appearance that bears no power, other than to offend a lower-ranking deputy. The absent deputy chief in charge of the jails, a position politics made up that didn't exist thirty years ago. The most significant problem with created appointed positions is they have no responsibility with endless authority. They make up their job duties as they go; their power comes from the sheriff. Since it's a ranking system, deputy chief direct every lesser ranking officer, meaning commanders down to officers, it's a position best given to a person who has been promoted through the ranks of the sheriff's office, but nepotism destroyed that practice.

Appointee, former clerk "Boy Sheriff", Robert Ficano, wasn't a police officer. Since he didn't come through the ranks of a police agency, he didn't care about the business of policing or police powers and what that meant. The Wayne County Sheriff's Office had a budget, and it was the beginning step to a higher position. He had his eye on a more important job than the sheriff. He was an attorney, a politician. Though, during those days, the system wasn't as micromanaged and there was only one deputy chief.

Sheriff Ficano didn't care about taking police powers unless it was necessary for news coverage. He would address things by necessity: that's where politics is won or lost. The sheriff's office was used more of a political stop on the way to county executive or some other higher position. For years, Robert Ficano and Patrick McNamara fought over the county executive seat. The county executive controls the budget in Wayne County. In 2003, Robert Ficano finally won the Wayne County Executive seat.

Warren Evans and Undersheriff, Larry Meyers came through the ranks. Larry Meyers followed Robert Ficano to the executive office, and the Undersheriff Daniel Pfannes appeared. Whether this appointment came by political favor or duress, no one knows. Under his charge, removing police power became commonplace, along with firing. Within his first year, twenty-eight officers were terminated; twenty-one won their jobs back through arbitration.

It's incredible to think in over eighteen years of my time at the sheriff's office, terminations and taking police powers weren't commonplace. One man comes on the scene; it turned into one to two deputies per month, terminated in his first year. It would appear that he was cleaning the house, but not when more than half won their positions back by arbitration.

These terminations are without pay, and when they win their jobs back, they have to fight to have pension, police powers, and back pay restored. The county doesn't give them back automatically but should. When you win in arbitration, you're right, that's just the beginning of a new fight. Before long, all this fighting exhaust you, and it seems you can't win, even though an arbitrator found the discharge was wrong and restored the officer.

Watching these injustices over the years affected my attitude. I grew to dislike how management would treat one mistake a decorated officer allegedly made. What's worse, the officer is never redeemed from the allegations, whether they are founded or unfounded. The punishment continues, essentially blackballed till they leave by retirement or go to another department.

I am not saying an officer shouldn't get terminated. There are actions that make one unfit for public service. But the same scrutiny used in hiring should be used for termination. When you take an inmate to the hospital, and he gets away and then, to add insult to injury, you lie like there are no cameras, termination is warranted. Another event that may lead to termination is getting into a fight and shooting someone because they made you angry, or worse, you are intoxicated

But the administration makes up unrealistic and unfair policies to justify terminating officers. In Duncan v. Wayne County Detroit, a deputy fell in love with a woman who was a family member of the undersheriff by marriage. The deputy breaks off his engagement with the woman and still get fired anyway (sounds personal?).

After that event, another deputy accepted a collect call from his brother, who was in prison and was terminated. His termination lasted over a year. He won his job back through arbitration, but still has not had his police power restored for taking a call from his incarcerated sibling. There are too many cases to cite, but the reality is it's a policy designed to control an already stressed workforce, best ran by robotics since people are prone to error.

In 2008, the undersheriff drafted a memo involving no contact with felons unless you receive permission from the undersheriff. It would seem that to some effect, this would be a civil rights issue. Still, because you work for these people, not the people of Wayne County, they can come up with any policy to justify structure and organizational soundness.

Now how this works is the plan is drafted, the sheriff signs off, and it becomes a law in the department. The sheriff doesn't read policies; he signs them. Fraternization with felons and police officers shouldn't happen, but when it a family member or personal relationship, it's so outrageous to think when you meet someone, you should ask, "Are you a felon? I better get permission from the undersheriff before we exchange numbers!"

# *Nkem*

Nkem was born in Nigeria, on the island of Bonny. The mother of Enyi, she too proclaimed to be a Christian. Was she? She showed up in my life as a financial advisor of Primerica. She claimed me as her adopted daughter, and so I would affectionately refer to her as my godmother or Nkem (mother in Igbo). Moved by her words, I embraced the idea since my mother rejected me.

I had prayed for a mature woman like the one Titus 2:3–5 speaks of; "The aged women likewise, teachers of good things; that they may teach the young women to be sober, to love their children, to be discreet, chaste, keepers at home, kind, obedient to their husband." I wanted to be married and beloved by my husband. But growing up in a single-parent family environment nurtured no experience for me to draw upon to function effectively in a marriage. I viewed Nkem as a teacher of good things.

## Priming for Financial Ruin

She helped by taking my youngest daughter to daycare in the morning. She paid for my other daughter to go to one of her son's graduation at a prestigious college. She would make herself available in situations of emergencies.

On one occasion, one of my daughters was taking an art class, and my other daughter was going to my mother's for the weekend so that I could work overtime without concern. I got in my jeep, and it wouldn't start. I called my mother, but she refused to help me because, as she put it, "It was rush hour, and I put my car up." I thought, is she serious! Put my car up! Putting up her car entailed parking it in the backyard. I hung up from her and called Nkem, with reservations since she had already had my youngest daughter all day. She said she was on her way, with no hesitation. My neighbor came over and cleaned my battery post before she got to my house, but I thought this lady came over here twice today; it was events like these that influenced me to trust and confide in her. Perhaps that was the plan!

I thought this was the mother I needed, little did I know everything she did or was doing was a setup for the kill. Ignorance is not bliss! As time passed and the relationship appeared to be growing, she asked me to review my retirement statements. Since she was a financial advisor, I thought her expertise would be of benefit to me. After she reviewed the documents, she asked me was I willing to invest some money with her, independent from my four-in-one pension.

In the beginning, she was spot on with the payments per month. So that developed a level of confidence in her. According to her, the plan was she would use my money to make money more than what the county could, and at the maturation of the loan, she could return the initial investment. It sounded like a good idea!

So, when she asked me to use a few of my credit cards, which should've been a red flag, I didn't overthink the request. I allowed her to use three of my credit cards and my retirement to my demise! I knew just enough about the Bible to make a wrong decision in love. The Bible says plenty to say about being a surety for strangers (Prov. 20:16 and 27:13, Amp.). The judge tells the creditors to take the garment of one who is security for a stranger and hold him in pledge when he is security for foreigners. But she wasn't a foreigner or stranger, I thought!

## Credit Denied

In October 2005, one of my dogs got sick, and I applied for credit to cover the bill and was denied. I had never been denied credit before. A couple of months before this, I asked her to stop using the cards and pay them off. She said okay, and I thought nothing more of the cards since, until then, she had been a woman of her word.

I called Nkem and asked her what was going on with the cards she was using. She told me she stopped paying the credit cards because of financial hardships, or so she claimed. Initially, I thought this wasn't so bad because it was only three cards with low limits, that's what I allowed her to use.

Little did I know it was far worse than what I anticipated. I wasn't aware she was using a total of eight cards, not three! She had used my personal information to open five additional credit cards without my knowledge. I was devastated when I found out. I couldn't believe this lady that claimed to be a Christian, and called me "daughter", had done this to me.

How she could do this to me and my children. She had not just taken from me; she took from my children, and that was the one thing that shook me the most. My daughters, as far as I was concerned, had already suffered enough. The following Sunday, after the credit card dilemma, I served at church. I shared my heaviness with one of my sisters.

After church, I called Nkem; I needed an explanation. I was surprised by the way she responded to me. When I asked her how did these cards become so many, she said, "Grace, no need to cry over spilled milk."

I started thinking maybe my sister at church was right; I may want to think about protecting myself and call a lawyer. I began to view Nkem as insincere. She had gotten money from me on so many occasions based on some investment idea. Now she was saying she wasn't sure what happened. I said, "I should've never blindly trusted you." Sure, I may have offended her, but really how do you know God and misuse people that trust you.

I began to wonder if that her original intent. She wasn't a young woman. She was well in her fifties, a grandmother. I began to think, was I just a job for her? I was more hurt, then angry. What she had done to me, no overtime would be enough to fix. Only God's grace could fill this gap in my heart and finances.

# Credit Card Lesson Began

That following Monday, I contacted an attorney. I explained how the relationship started and how I trusted this lady and allowed her to use a few of my credit cards and that she opened five more accounts without my knowledge or permission. She had credit cards in my name in various combinations with my ex-husbands' last names; for example, Edith Wilson, Grace Mills-Wilson. It was crazy! I didn't know banks or credit card companies would issue cards like that. All these credit cards were going to her house, and she was paying them until she changed her mind, ran out of money, or was done misusing my name; only God knows what her real reason was.

To clear my credit report was a five-year process. When she opened the additional accounts and paid on them for a few years, the companies thought I just decided not to pay. The process to prove I didn't live at that address was an arduous one. Where I had arrived emotionally after that conversation with Nkem the day before caused me to pursue the unthinkable protection for myself.

I filed a police report for the cards I didn't authorize. I made payment arrangements for the cards I allowed her to use and sent her a letter to cease using my name to obtain credit. I sent it registered mail, which she never signed for, but she got the message the credit card scam was over. I learned banks only keep records for seven years: seven years from the date you're inquiring of which meant for me I couldn't retrieve banking information from the inception of the five credit card accounts. The companies were coming at me hard since it appeared I was paying, then just abruptly stop paying them.

Regardless of filing police reports, they wanted me to pay since I had a job, one rep told me. I felt so stupid during this process, trying to explain myself to these people; this was identity theft. I just knew the thief! I learned they couldn't garnish me because I filed a police report, and I notified the credit card companies of who she was and what she had. I never lived at that address: I just had to prove it. I was stumped for a while because these people kept calling me. I kept praying for help, being ignorant, and thinking the best of this lady landed me in a place; I didn't know how or where recovery would show up.

What had I allowed by letting this person to use my credit?! Gave her permission to do everything she did. The relationship her went places it had no business going. Had she been God-fearing, it wouldn't have. I honestly believed that she had my best interest at heart, and she wouldn't do anything to hurt my daughters or me: man was I so wrong! She knew my vulnerabilities, my recent divorce, my relationships with my family members, or the lack thereof and particularly my relationship with my mother.

Was It a Sarcastic Remark? Or a Teaching Moment?

Nkem knew I had very few friends. My priority was my daughters; so when she said to me one day, "Your closest friend is your ex-husband's wife," I thought, Why is she saying this to me? In retrospect, she was sizing me up to destroy me.

Although Sam and I were divorced, we had a daughter together. I saw the necessity to have a relationship with his wife. Vanessa reached out to me to get to know my daughter and spend time together as a family. I had no insecurities about my position with my daughters. I welcomed a relationship that would be good for my daughter. I'm sure Nkem may have surmised that from how often I spoke with Sam's wife, she was what I considered a close friend. Single parenting was my life. I didn't have many friends. But I never viewed that as a weakness or strength. It was what it was. I worked, took care of my children, and took them to church. I didn't view my life as a negative.

Except on the occasional birthday dinner with a few ladies from work: we would take turns treating each other for our birthdays to dinner. It started as fun a few ladies getting together to celebrate! That event soon turned into "I needed to do something other than going to work and church; I needed a man in my life." I thought, for what? I'm good! I stop participating in the birthday dinners; I just wasn't interested in a relationship at that time, nor was I interested in defending my position.

Nkem taught me many lessons; one was never to let people use your credit. They may mean well, but let's face it, sometimes unplanned events happen! This whole credit thing and allowing someone to use your worth is risky business, a mortgage: death pledge on your future. My longing for love deceived me. Did she see my financial value and went to work? Opening accounts, cashing in on my weaknesses?

I believe so, but I refuse to let this event make me bitter. In retrospect, I felt she had only done what my natural mother had done to me. I wanted to learn from this not be condemned by this violation of trust. Even so, I wondered was all her time spent with me a gathering of intel to use for her benefit later? Was every conversation for the express purpose to see my thoughts and heart on things?

I once shared with her how one of my co-workers, who I considered a friend, told that she thought I was stupid because I received her advice and then turned around and did the opposite of what she suggested. She realized I wasn't slow-witted. I explained to my friend if the thing you advise makes sense, why not do it? However, if the idea didn't make sense, why do it? She said, but if the person (speaking of herself) thinks they can tell you what to do because you take their advice, you fool them; she said that's pretty smart.

I felt so taking advice is stupid. Okay, that's your opinion! And besides, I felt my friend was speaking more about her inadequacies than my shortcomings. That was just one of the many conversations I shared with her. These types of communications revealed to her, I had no friends and what others thought of me. Making me her prey for her future use, before this situation, I didn't think of females as predatory types; she taught me we could be for a little of money.

## Power of Relationships

I held on to what the Word of God says about love in 1 Corinthians 13:5 (Amp). It is not conceited; it is not rude and does not act unbecomingly. Love (God's love in us) does not insist on its way, for it is not self-seeking; it is not touchy or fretful or resentful; it takes no account of the evil done to it (it pays no attention to a suffered wrong). Crushed and devastated to tears could do no justice for this travesty. The services rendered, I thought, were for love but were simply for money. I didn't get mad. I was so hurt!

I sought God for wisdom and took to working overtime (couldn't take time to feel sorry for myself) to pay the cards I let her use and returned my tithes, believing for the grace of God to manifest in this situation.

The greatest gift I got from this betrayal, yes, I said gift, is to love my daughters. Sure, I loved them, but this situation put things into perspective. The lack of relationship with my mother left this gaping hole in my development. I must have a relationship with my daughters, love them despite themselves, be there, and pray for them unceasingly. I wanted to be the woman in Titus for my daughters.

Had my mother been able to be there (spiritually and emotionally), Nkem would have never gotten close to me, or my daughters. She knew my daughters were my primary concern. She once said to me, "All you care about in your daughters." I thought, wasn't I suppose too! Between my father, that wasn't there, and my mother stating she never wanted me and telling me about it until I was eighteen years old, I developed within me a personal dysfunction that anyone that got close could see. I thought the right relationship would nurture me to a place of completion, which was true.

That relationship was and is in Jesus Christ. Ekong told me about the tribe where Nkem was from. He described them as masters of deception for financial gain and would sell their mother for the right price. He wasn't any better, though! Nkem promised to pay back the money she received for investments and loans.

## The Best Advice from the Bible

God's Word is clear on the consequences of being credit for another person (Proverbs 27:13 and 20:16) Co-signing, allowing someone to use your credit is not wise and void of understanding (Proverbs 17:18). Apart from knowing these words on two occasions, the Holy Spirit warned me a small voice disturbed my peace when she asked me to invest.

On one of those occasions, I am sure she heard my reluctance. I told her I must pray. I hung up the phone, and before I could get into my prayer, she called back. I should've completed my prayer, then called her back. My ignorance prompted me to answer the phone. She said, "Well, you know I am a Christian." I replied, "Yes, I do."

That was a red flag! Why would someone need to say that? Jesus said in Matthew 7:16, "Ye shall know them by their fruits."

That distraction of the enemy and my ignorance allowed spiritual bullying to support the idea of a so-called Christian. Every time she asked for money for investments, I had a Holy Spirit prompting a sense of caution in my solar plexus area. But I held on to the idea of "love is believing the best." Stupid, not trusting the warning I was experiencing in my gut. I didn't adhere to that caution. I didn't understand God's leading or love for me; he personally and intimately cares about every area of my life. God's grace walked my daughters and me through, losing our garment as described in Prov. 20:16 and Prov. 27:13. Love, the love of God, does not take advantage of the weakness of others (1 Corinthians 13:5).

## ❧ CHAPTER 16 ❧

# *2011*

## Joseph Prince

For years, I felt like I wasn't good enough. Only when I came to know how much God loves me and what all happened at the cross with Jesus Christ did God's forgiveness seem possible. That revelation came through my partnership with Joseph Prince Ministries.

Some years later, I had another Holy Spirit rendezvous. I asked my Heavenly Father for growth and development since he would not release me from my present church. I needed something, and that something was to see more of Jesus, the grace of God.

While at work, channel surfing in my office, I heard this man say "Jesus Christ". He was dressed rather casual for a preacher, but he said, "Jesus Christ," and the way he said it had passion and meaning. That man was Joseph Prince. It was through his ministry that elucidated and rightly dividing the scriptures came alive for me.

That was a whole new world for me; sure, I knew scriptures, but much of what I knew was in the style of the law. I frequently left church feeling like I need to do better! Because I heard from the pulpit, "We need to do better." The law condemns, "Grace gives life" is what I was hearing.

Whenever I listened to Joseph Prince, I would get to church and understand, "I needed to do better." I was perplexed. The present leadership of the church I was attending always reminded the congregation that "he wasn't a perfect man and that we needed to pray for our pastor," so that's what I did daily! I prayed that the first family would come to know the grace of God, Jesus Christ and preach that truth, not just the Bible.

Daily listening to Joseph Prince in the morning and throughout the day and reading my Bible, gave permanence to the Word of God. A continuity based on the blood of Jesus, just as Jesus cannot unshed his blood. My position in Christ Jesus will not change (that consciousness gave me boldness in approaching the throne of God: Hebrews 4:16). I am in an eternal place of the righteousness of God in Christ Jesus (Romans 5:21). My full standing with God rests on Jesus Christ. God's unchanging love for me sits on the finished works of Jesus Christ at the cross, not my vacillating heart or mind. God the Father sees me in Christ, Jesus, and Jesus is perfect. All my spiritual exhaustion and insecurities melt away in that truth.

In 2011, I was restless and wanted to leave the church I was attending. I understood God's position on the under-shepherd (pastor or bishop) and leaving where God placed me wasn't a decision to be entered into lightly. I needed God's direction. I prayed and got no release, so I stayed regardless of my feelings of restlessness. In hindsight, I realize my Heavenly Father did not want me outside the church, seeking for a church, but inside, seeking Jesus; it wasn't that where I was, was so terrible.

It changed leadership, and I was having difficulties adjusting to the change. Although, when the previous shepherd returned, the state of my heart was still in a state of unrest. Through that, I learned restlessness isn't a time for a change, but a time for growth. Had I left prematurely, I would've missed out on a stage in spiritual development.

Those we need to do better sermons bothered me because if I can do better, why would Jesus need to die for me. Jesus did it all, he did all those things I couldn't do for myself, and He is still doing those things I cannot do for myself, at the right hand of God. He makes perfect my imperfect prayers (Romans 8:34).

All I heard was Jesus Christ, his entire sermon highlighted Jesus Christ. That man was Joseph Prince. Jesus Christ, and the finished work at the cross is all he kept referring to. Everything changed for me as a believer: I am a new creation, because of the finished works of Jesus Christ. I am righteousness, not perfect because I don't need to be. Jesus is. As Jesus is, so am I in this world. All I need to do is see more of Jesus in the reading, hearing and listening to God's word to bask in my Father's grace.

The Holy Spirit introduced me to this man (Joseph Prince) talking about Jesus Christ that day in my office, and four years later, I was traveling to see him preach in Singapore at his church! Traveling to Singapore in 2015 to visit New Creation Church took my level of thirst to know God and see more of Jesus Christ.

This church was magnificent, like nothing I've seen. This congregation was huge, but since I was in an assembly that was large for the metropolitan Detroit area, it wasn't intimating, but there was no comparison. I've always felt like a large church stands for the largeness of saints in Heaven.

This spiritual hiatus was a glance at the love of Father God: the goodness of God is much more than the daily benefit we see and have, it's eternal. Far too often, we say waking up in the morning is a blessing not to be taken for granted, and I agree, but it's bigger than getting up out of bed. Knowing you are the righteousness of God in Christ Jesus, this unchangeable position in God's eternal family is without repentance (Romans 11:29). Righteousness is a gift from God. God's abundant provision of grace and the gift of righteousness to reign in life through the one man, Jesus Christ (Romans 5:17).

## Child of God

Our position (the child of God) rest on the blood of Jesus. Without the shedding of blood there is no remission of sins (Hebrews 9:22); my salvation is based on the blood of Jesus, not just my confession and not based on my good works. Not to say I can live a sinful lifestyle while confessing, "I'm a child of God." They don't go together.

The problem with sin is bondage. Man in captivity can't reign in life, and God wants man to reign in life. Sure, God has promised never to leave nor forsake us (Hebrews 13:5), but that's not permission to live as if Jesus Christ isn't Lord of your life. Being in a relationship with Jesus Christ governs every area of your life.

God isn't just God; he is my Father. I'm in the family of God I don't need to be perfect with family, I need to receive the love of my Father! The Father's love and favor for me doesn't change since I did nothing to earn it. All I got to do is live in the consciousness I am the righteousness of God in Christ Jesus, because of the finished works of Jesus Christ at the cross (2 Corinthians 5:21):my daily confession. Just as Jesus isn't coming off the cross, I am forever righteous.

My sins, whatever they are, are not more significant than the blood of Jesus. My salvation rests on my confession and the blood of Jesus Christ; it's his blood; that's where my forgiveness and redemption are assured. Not my works or ideas of doing good. I've learned I can do all the right things for the wrong reasons.

The perfect example I could think of is in Luke 21:1–4, the widow that gave two mites Jesus said she cast in more than they all: for all these have offered from their abundance, she gave all, she gave of her heart.

## CHAPTER 17

# Jail Break, God Protects

On January 20, 2012, I was leaving work. I would park my vehicle in the garage of Jail Division 2; I felt I wasn't alone that day. No, let me go back; this wasn't the beginning of this incident for me. My morning routine consisted of praying, reading the Bible, and listening to Joseph Prince as I got dressed. One morning during meditation, "I heard inmate garage running." I thought, what's that and that can't be. My thinking was it's January there no basketball playing; inmates don't go outside. So I thought! My reasoning stood in the way of inquiring of Father God for revelation. Almost to my detriment, failing to sit before Him nearly cost me my life. After meditation, I went to work as always, forgetting the words the Holy Spirit spoke to me, and not being sure what they meant. I was working overtime in abundance; was that the reason for missing the Holy Spirit? Or was it a matter of my development in my relationship with Him? Not sure, but it was the Holy Spirit with me in that garage that protected me that afternoon.

Friday, January 20, 2012, as I was leaving work walking to my car, I remember feeling a little eerie. I discounted it; it was the weekend I spent time taking care of my great-nephew. I looked around in the garage, didn't see anything or anyone. I quickly got into my car and locked the doors. As I drove through the parking lot, before reaching Gratiot Avenue, I looked to the right first for pedestrians, then to my left for cars.

When I looked to the left, I saw an inmate running out of the garage. I immediately got this sinking feeling in my gut, thinking, oh no, this was the warning! I called Jail Division 2 shift command as I followed this inmate. The following ended at a restaurant called Coach's Corner; he ran in, and there he disappeared.

Once I called shift command, it seemed like all the police in downtown Detroit become a part of this search of recapturing the inmate. He was found hiding in a dumpster behind the restaurant. In the process of this chase, I damaged the front tire of my car, called AAA, and returned to jail. My lieutenant told me, "I may have to write you up." I asked, "For what?" He said, "For leaving early." I said, "Ask the midnight shift sergeants who relieved them, and at what time?" I arrived early out of habit and saw no harm in letting the midnight shift leave twenty to thirty minutes early.

I couldn't believe this treatment was my reward; instead of a commendation, I would have to answer for leaving work early that day. By the end of the day, an executive commander took credit for chasing down the escapee. That same operational commander assisted in giving me more duties the following week. The credit of recapturing the escapee went to an executive commander when it was a team effort. I didn't get a write-up for leaving early; I guess I should've been happy. The threat of a reprimand was only the beginning of this foolishness.

When returning to the jail, I drafted the conduct incident reports (write-ups) for the officers assigned to garage recreation that day. The lieutenant said to me you can't do that. My response was why. He said, "It's an investigation." I thought, really!? Since when did an incident occur, and no reports are generated? Little did I understand that neither group of officers performed a headcount, the floor security officer (special friends of the lieutenant), or the transporting officers of recreation. If I wrote up the officers under my charge, the floor security sergeants would have had to write up their officers.

The two black deputies assigned to garage recreation were reassigned for a few months, then moved back with no discipline incurred. The two white floor security officers that failed to make a headcount received nothing. It took me three months to get the department to pay for the damages to my tire, and even then, they reduced it to a prorated payout.

I was a little melancholy about this situation. The people I work with every day were acting in ways that I couldn't and didn't want to believe. I learned that wearing the same uniform means nothing; there is no unity in the outfit.

The following week of the garage escape incident, I observed a deputy chief, executive commander, lieutenant, and captain coming out of an office. The captain approached me and stated, "Starting Monday, you and your crew are to preform sanitation inspections during lunchtime." During lunchtime, I thought, how is that supposed to happen? No details were given. Nothing in writing. Just a verbal order.

The following Monday, I attempted to follow the rules. A situation where I should've received a commendation, I got more duties instead!

Before this escape happened in my unit, two of my male colleagues (both white) were involved in an inmate escape. They weren't assigned additional duties, because of officers under their charge failing to supervise their inmates properly.

In one of those cases, the deputies didn't secure the inmate before taking him for medical treatment, and the prisoner was at large for thirty hours. That escape happened in January 2011; the department terminated the deputies. The sergeant collected reports.

In my incident, the deputies didn't receive a written reprimand; they got temporarily reassigned for a few months and returned to the unit—while the rest of my officers and I were performing sanitation inspections! It would appear they got away with this indiscretion.

The following Monday of the escape, one of the deputies assigned to the garage detail was smiling big during roll call. I felt a bit taunted by this big grin, but I just addressed the troops during roll call and carried on with regular business.

Deep within me, I knew the Holy Spirit warned me about this event. I didn't feel condemned; I felt more of I missed the mark, but this smiling deputy seemed unapologetic. But the lesson I learned that day was to say nothing; let God continue to be Lord in this situation. It wasn't easy, being her supervisor. Still, my position was given to me by God, not man, and at that moment, I knew it was Father God that protected in me that garage, not luck or chance, but my Heavenly Father.

The following year, on the same day, this same deputy was involved in another inmate escape. An inmate was bonded out, but it wasn't the correct inmate. The inmates switched armbands on the ward; the one that got out was a federal inmate. That resulted in the federal government taking all their prisoners out of the downtown jails.

Was she fatigued from overtime, or had she fell into a routine of trusting inmates? She called out an inmate, one stepped out, but the wrong one. Just as she failed to perform a headcount the year before, this time, she failed to check the armband of the inmate that stepped off the ward. I felt sorry for her because now the department was going to address the loss. After all, it was a federal inmate.

The escape that happened the year before the recaptured was almost immediate. There was no real loss to the department, and because of some benefiting factors, she appeared to have come out unscathed. She was notorious for telling everyone she was a Christian but operated in complete disregard for others' safety. I was sorry that her lesson came at such a considerable price.

Nevertheless, had the department disciplined her for the first escape, the second one may not have happened. But the department felt that the supervisor, should be assigned additional duties for the failure of these officers to perform a proper count. Was this disparity in treatment based on race or sex? I couldn't figure out what made me a subject of additional duties under similar circumstances of departmental infractions. My guess was it was my gender, or my permanent tan. I didn't want to think my treatment resulted from my skin color or gender. It seems like such a crutch to use. But the department over the years has shown a disparity in treatment based on gender or race.

That was a challenging year for me. I spoke to my union steward about the issue, which was unsuccessful. According to the union, management could do everything they were doing. Everything was within my classification. Never mind the condition that brought about the additional duties. Regardless of the apparent disparage in treatment, along with being assigned to two separate jail faculties.

I attempted to conduct the sanitation inspections during lunchtime, as ordered. At lunch, the holding cells are attorney's booth to visit their clients. These were the same cells needed during sanitation inspection. The inmates are escorted off the ward and placed in the hallway holding cells. I went to the captain that initially gave me the detail. I asked him, "Why is it that every time changes come about to my unit or units? I'm not in those meetings?" He replied, "You wouldn't be." I replied, perplexed, "No disrespect, sir, but why? Is it because of my gender or the color of my skin?" He replied, "I don't see it that way." I responded, "Of course, not you're a white man." He turned beet red.

I excused myself before I received a conduct incident report for insubordination, which wasn't my intent at all. A few hours later, I was called by the only black female commander in the department to report to her office. She told me, "You can't talk to the captain like that." I replied, "Well, if we don't have the practice to substantiate my allegation, we're fine. However, if we do, then that's you all problem." I asked her, "How am I supposed to perform these lunchtime sanitation inspections?" She said, "I don't know, but you better figure it out before you get in trouble." With that good advice, I excused myself from her office.

There was no policy for this new detail to punish the recreation staff for this escape, just a standing order of you will follow your last order, whatever that is. The function of inmates seeing their attorneys outweighed performing these lunchtime ward searches. The inspections that started never got completed due to attorney visits: can't cancel or deny an attorney the right to see his client. The process of starting and stopping inspections was frustrating, and I met no solution until I went to the Equal Employment Opportunity Commission. My thinking was, let's see who does the shakedowns when I'm not here; if this is a must-to-do assignment, who will the lieutenant assign this crucial task?

When I was on vacation in December for three weeks during the Christmas vacation, no other sergeant was assigned the task of performing the sanitation inspections. No sanitation inspection for three weeks spoke to the necessity of the function. The EEOC ruled the county wasn't asking anything out of my job classification. The department changed the function back to a floor security function, which was what it was in the first place, so basically I won.

## ❧ CHAPTER 18 ❧

# *Ekong: My Third Marriage*

After thirteen years of being single and promising to remain single, I met a man who claimed he was a born-again Christian. Nigerian raised, but a United States citizen, Ekong was the son of a chief of the providence. He grew up in an upper-class home according to Nigerian standards. He was a very charming man with a flowery speech. He returned to the United States as an adult.

It wasn't long before he found himself in the criminal justice system for fraud. He told me it was his mother who taught him the fraudulent business of check cashing. I wondered if these people came to this country to exploit the trust woven into the people of the church and the financial institutions. They represent themselves as Christian or Muslim to cash in on the trust factor in that belief system.

I still wanted to believe the very best of people. I tried because I always felt in my profession, I saw the worse of people and situations. That thinking became a fault for me, since I would look away from the negative to see the positive.

I inquired of the Lord when I was serious about marrying this man, and the one thing I got was "WAIT," but I didn't listen. Now, the "wait" I was experiencing, I dismissed as well since I was single for thirteen years. Maybe, I am just afraid to commit, and he told me he was a Christian. We would make a good team. In the back of my mind was the birthday crew saying, "You need a man in your life."

He said, "I'm not committing crime anymore." I believed him; who enjoys going to jail? He coached me into thinking I had inhibitions because I was single for many years, which made sense. Second-guessing myself was wrong thinking! I knew it would be a challenge. The courtship was brief; I had neglected to spend the necessary time before God, to ascertain proper direction.

I allowed this man to press me, saying I was his ministry, and he was mine, telling me I needed to be with someone and that we could have a good life together. He was a man with religious trappings, so I believed he knew God.

He spoke scripture; we attended church, watched Dr. Creflo Dollar on TV, brought CDs and DVDs of religious programming, and purchased different versions of the Bible for study. He did just about everything to lead me to believe he was seeking God's will for his life, and since we were a couple, he was praying for the family. He claimed to pray for at least an hour and a half before starting his workday. He played the role of being on fire for God.

He was honest, in the beginning, he told me about his criminal record, but said he "was done with that lifestyle." He told me he might have two children in New York and possibly two in Michigan, but he had no paternity results. In hindsight, I must have been crazy. My daughters said I was in love, but I had made commitments before, and I did not want to give up so easy this time. I stayed longer than I should have. We did counseling, twice; once in the beginning, and once after I filed for divorce. Deep within, I didn't want to divorce again.

## Revelation in Marriage #3

I can't get married again. Is my behavior making a mockery out of my Father's precious institution (marriage)? The chain of events that kept me and protected me was the GRACE OF GOD. This man, I learned from his mother, had devastated every woman's life he crossed paths with, except me. That was God's grace. I ignored the Holy Spirit's leading. I wanted to believe not all people in the region practice the same habits.

I didn't understand people from third world countries were raised with an entirely different set of standards, even if they are Christians. America is a land of opportunity, and the whole world knows that is why people from all over the world want to come here. In America, we have freedom, disagree amicably, vote, and the winner stays in office for a term. We don't plan a coup and raid the White House or Capitol Hill to take control (well, most of the time). We wait for our turn and strategize for political change.

## Religion versus Christianity

I learned in this third marriage—the actual difference between religion and Christianity. Religion is bondage, a rigid way of thinking and believing, and Christianity is freedom. Jesus came that we might have life and have it more abundantly (John 10:10). Christianity is a lifestyle where Jesus is Lord. Holiness is the order of your lifestyle because it is a fruit of grace and not a result of fleshly works or effort. God's living word is the order of the day.

## A Religious Man

I married this man and ignored the "wait" led of the Holy Spirit. For five and a half years, I lived in a state of uncertainty, at times, downright miserable. Yes, every Sunday, we went to church and some Wednesdays, but it was all an act. This man would go to church, claim Christianity, but when meeting a Muslim, he would greet them with "As-Salaam-Alaikum." I asked him why he did that as a Christian, he would say its business. I thought to myself, what kind of game is that? To greet a person in their vernacular when you are not of that religious culture seemed a little deceptive.

We argued this point one night to no avail, he continued to practice his deception, little did I know, I too was being deceived, and God was protecting me. The man was showing me who he was I didn't want to believe what he was showing me. He started an international trading company. We went to the Hong Kong Electronic

Fair several times from 2007 to 2009. In 2008, we went to a trade-show in Dubai.

After several trips to these exotic places, I suggested to this man to get a regular job to support the family. Since the traveling to trade shows wasn't netting a profit or securing a contract, which would provide an avenue for future income. The trips were entertaining, and I learned a lot but were fruitless ventures. He went from an international import-export business to solar energy business. He never received contracts with any of these ideas.

He told me he had money overseas, which I never saw. The solar business started with a trip to an energy conference in Munich, Germany. Then he found out about Solar Energy Institute in Carbondale, Colorado. We went there for solar installation and other types of energy sources like wind. Solar Energy Institute offered more opportunities for him to travel, and because I wanted to be with him, I went too.

We went to Ecuador and stayed at Rio Muchacho, an organic farm to experience installing solar panels. Making a bicycle pedal power water pump system. Confusing, I know! The idea was to generate electricity that would store in a back-up battery system for the solar panels. It sounded like too much! It was!

While there, he accused me of wanting some guy in our tour group. I took a horse ride on a mare that had recently given birth. The colt walked alongside the momma horse. That was cute! The problem was her stallion followed also. Ekong thought I was flirting with the man was riding the stallion since it appeared he and I were together when the horses were following each other.

After that, it seemed to him every time he turned around, the guy on the horse was looking for me around the farm. What confused me about this madness was why he let the man hang around us. I wondered was it because we were the only people of color on this farm or was my husband afraid of the guy.

It was this trip to Ecuador, where I began to question, "Does this man love me?" He argued with me in this foreign place where he was the only person I knew or could talk to. I couldn't call anyone in this remote place. But this was the third time he had behaved this way, the first time was in Dubai, the second time was in Hong Kong. These weren't just an exchange of words resulting from a disagreement. He was cruel.

In Dubai, he spoke harshly to me, because I asked him for money to buy a necklace, which I promised to repay once we got home. Since that was the first time, he verbally checked out on me. My feelings were hurt. He apologized later and brought me a necklace, and since that was the first time, I set my mind to forget the incident.

## Beginning of the End

In January 2011, we went to Jamaica to celebrate my birthday. When we returned home from the birthday celebration, we booked a cruise for May. While giving the travel agent our passport numbers, I noticed he had two passport stamps for the Philippines, one at the end of 2010 and another in January 2011.

In March, I went to see an attorney and filed for divorce. I felt I needed to protect myself from whatever this man was doing. That scared me because he never told me, and I thought, what was the nature of this so-called business he could have had over there. Whatever the reason could have been, I didn't want any part of it, whether it was drugs, money, or women.

The thought of this guy is leaving the country doing God knows what, with God knows who. It was too much. I was tired of this game of deception! I reached a point of pure fatigue in 2011; it was at this point of exhaustion that opened my eyes to this man.

When he was booking trips around the world, he failed to pay the taxes on the house. How I found out was an entire sequence of events: he stole my gas card. Since I didn't use my gas card all the time, I'm sure he thought he could put it back before I noticed it was gone (this whole incident was God's Grace in effect). My custom was to use cash for gas on pay week and use the card on non-pay weeks, to hold on to my money. He didn't know my thinking behind using it.

# Blinders Removed

When the credit card resurfaced, I called his mother, a God-fearing woman, the same woman that he claims taught him his nefarious trade. I told her about the recent activities, and she told me, "Get all your checks out of the house, that probably isn't the only thing he has done." I shared my pain over these recent events with her and how he wrote bogus checks on my account, and I couldn't believe this man would steal from his own family. But I don't think he viewed my daughters and me as family.

When I got off the phone with her, it was that still small voice that whispered to me, "Check the taxes." I went and discovered I was two weeks from foreclosure. I made a payment arrangement and trusted God. I called Ekong and questioned him about the taxes, not mentioning the gas card. The house taxes were pressing; the gas card wasn't.

When Ekong failed to pay the taxes, it was my mother that gave me the money to stop the foreclosure. During one of my phone calls her, I shared how he was supposed to pay the taxes but had not and that I was days from foreclosure. His mother, my mother, our conversations and God's grace saved my daughter's and me from dire straits. My mother asked me how much money did you need. I told her "You can't help me." She asked me again. I said, "Maybe my brother can help me." She said again, "How much money do you need?" I told her how much it was, and she said, "Come over here and I'm going to give you an apron." As bad I felt from having to go to my mother, she loaned me the money and Ekong paid it back.

The irony of it all was that he had this unassuming way about him. As if he was so intelligent and righteous, just a person beyond reproach. He would seldom apologize for his nefarious activity.

He called "business" writing bad checks and using other people's names to make purchases. An identity thief is what he was. Printing currency or allowing others to do it is counterfeiting and facilitating criminal activity. The printing money prompted me to call the federal government. It wasn't business; it was an illegal activity. I shared my concerns with my brother. He said, "You needed to call the feds yesterday. That man is a fool!"

It was God's grace; this man showed me this counterfeit money. When I called the federal government, they came to my work location and interviewed me. I was embarrassed, but I couldn't have the federal government performing a raid on my house looking for counterfeit securities. I had entirely too much to lose; embarrassment was a small price to pay for such a colossal mistake. God's grace protected me!

While all this was going on, we were attending church as a couple. I prayed, and I wanted this marriage to work, but I grew exhausted with him. His arguing and finding fault in everything and everyone, and his atrocious activities were too much. This man wanted to be a criminal and I couldn't stop him. My prayers changed to God protect my household from his "business" activity.

The interview with the federal government eventually led to his indictment for facilitating fraudulent activity involving counterfeit money and checks. He appeared to operate a legitimate business in the Ford Building in downtown Detroit while printing fraudulent checks and money. The agent in charge told me they were already watching this crew of people circulating counterfeit cash in the area: buying stuff like televisions, computers, and copiers.

Once the federal government performed the raid at the Ford Building. This Ekong found another location in downtown Detroit, a workspace, not an office like what he had in the Ford Building. I attempted to have the divorce papers served several times, unsuccessfully. Of course, I told him I filed. Regardless of what he was doing, I still didn't want him to be surprised by my decision to end this madness.

As much as I wanted to trust and believe him, I couldn't any longer! I needed to put space between us and end the association. Not only was he not a man of God, but he was a criminal. I'm sure he viewed people as prey. People had no value for him other than to misuse them.

There was a guy that would hang around at his office, which I'll call Jesse. Jesse had a criminal record. I thought no big deal, but Jesse didn't just have a criminal past. He was still working on his criminal record. So, this guy being a practicing criminal, I asked my husband, "Why are you hanging out with him?" He would say, "Grace, I'm trying to help the man," and I repeatedly told him, "You can't! You have a criminal history too." Little did I know Jesse was helping him print counterfeit cash!

## Dead Man, Not Dead?

As a police officer, it would seem I would check on Law Enforcement Network System, but that's against the law. It's illegal to use Law Enforcement Network Systems for personal use. Although, when everything was said and done, I wished I did!

I wasn't the only one slipping when it came to this character. The federal government was too. Ekong was guy listed as deceased on record. He and I had been out of the country several times. He lost his passport twice and was issued another, but according to federal records, he was deceased. According to the agent, the death certificate was received by fax from his mother, but the name of the sender was not his mother, it was one of the mothers of his children! I was shocked!

I said to the agent, "So let me get this right, he's dead according to your records?" She confirmed. I thought, no wonder we got a terrorist problem in this country when we give dead men passports. No one could have told me our government would issue a United States passport to a dead man! The bright side of this for me was at least he wouldn't be out until trial, arguing with me and committing more crimes. With this new fraudulent revelation, he was ineligible for a bond.

When he got himself locked up, that was the first peace I had in years. This man would fuss at me if the dog came in the bathroom with me. He quarreled with me if my daughter's boyfriend came over and God forbid, he was there till dark. He would have a conniption if he didn't get served dinner before everyone else, while always perched in front of the bedroom television. He argued and found fault in anything and everything I did!

Ekong bickered so much I couldn't remember why I was attracted to him in the first place! On two separate occasions, he hit me. The first time my brother came home from prison and would visit often, too much for him, but that was my brother for crying out loud! His excuse that time was, he said, "I was tired of taking the mess off your family." I did not know what mess he was talking about. My oldest brother was the only one visiting me. He apologized after I had a conversation with his mother.

The second time came after Marcus was exonerated. Surely, he didn't think I wanted to get back with him. By the time Marcus was released, we hadn't spoken in over ten years! I had no interest in him. I felt sorry for him and was concerned about whether he could adjust to a free society.

He said to me, "You looked funny when you saw him and your daughter on television." He hit me and tried to get me on the bed. I fought back this time because I felt if he accomplished getting me on the bed, I might end up dead. Eventually, I got away from him and ran out the back door. He packed up some clothes and left. A few days later, he apologized to my daughters and me. He never hit me again after that, but the memory lived on in the back of my mind because he seemed to enjoy fighting.

There was little difference between the verbal and physical fighting; they both hurt. This relationship was the most painful of all my marriages, and once I got exhausted, I started evaluating my life. I needed peace. Initially when he was incarcerated, I intended to be supportive to him, regardless of the impending divorce. I loved him; I couldn't be his wife any longer. I would send him money and accept phone calls until one evening I had a nightmare.

In the dream, he was attacking me. The phone calls from him turned into arguments. I refused to visit; I worked in a jail. The nightmare woke me up to the reality of this guy is mean, selfish, and I couldn't take it anymore. Not even a month before he went to jail, he approached me and said, "You know you fifty, don't nobody want you, but to use you." I just looked at him and thought, what does that got to do with anything? Then it was as if a light came on.

He thought I was with him because I needed to be with someone. I laughed, and he asked me what was funny.

I said, "Oh, you thought I was with you because I needed to be with someone? No, I was with you because I wanted to be with you."

"You're full of yourself," he said.

"Which one is it? I'm fifty and don't anybody want me, or I'm full of myself." I guess because I wasn't crying anymore, he walked away. His words had no power anymore.

Who Was This Man? Who Did I Marry?

In the summer of 2012, while cleaning my garage, I came across a black bag. It wasn't mine; it was unfamiliar, so I looked inside. In the bag were papers belonging to Ekong: paternity papers for his children in Michigan. He said he never got the test results for them. The other documents were of prior criminal cases: check cashing and statements naming him as the leader in a check-cashing ring.

Other papers listed his wife's name, dated 2004, the same name as the woman on the fraudulent death certificate. Was she still his wife when we got married? We married in December 2005, the guy told me he was divorced, was he? Did they fake the death certificate to collect on life insurance? So many papers of his past nefarious activities. I stop looking as I was overwhelmed at a depth of the deception, fraud, lying, and cheating. Who was this guy!?

I thought, who does this type of stuff? How foolish was I to believe this guy? I had to remind myself: God loves me, and my position in Christ Jesus didn't change because I missed the mark. It's easy for me to condemn myself in the face of all this. God's love is more significant than my mistakes!

Only God knows. I never demanded that this man prove himself, I should have, I took him at his word. Even God says "Prove me now," although God is talking about the tithe and offerings (Mal. 3:10). He's still speaking of showing himself faithful to his word. Since the creator of heaven and earth says, "try me" that is a standard, not just in money matters, but in life matters. Evidence for me that it's perfectly acceptable to require someone to prove themselves, and when love is involved, it should be a welcomed activity for both parties. The things

I am sure of in the aftermath of this madness, God protected me; he carried me and sheltered me. I know God loves ME.

## God Silence Meant to Rest and Wait!

When I prayed about this marriage, God was silent after I heard "wait", I didn't know or understand God's silence, so I received it as acceptance or approval in my ignorance and immaturity. I took this man at his word. Cursed be the man that trusts in man, whose heart departs from the Lord (Jer. 17:5). I didn't intend to go away from the Lord, but that is what I did when I married that man.

He said he grew up in West Africa, accepted Christ at a young age, and received divine healing when someone forced him to drink battery acid. He knew scripture, but so does Lucifer. He appeared sincere, and I like to believe the best of people. I know the "wait" was for revelation, to give him time to prove himself. My taking him at his word cost me big time. I got to pay bills I didn't make, which meant I gave money to some already wealthy people.

I got to waste precious time, which should have been fulfilling God's purpose for my life. God never made a woman take care of man; she's a helpmate. I didn't spend enough time seeking God to ascertain God's will for my life. The silence was an opportunity for me to spend more time with my Heavenly Father and do absolutely nothing but rest and wait for him to answer.

## ✥ CHAPTER 19 ✥

# *My Choices*

In 1917, Katharine Cook Briggs she embarked on a project of reading biographies. Subsequently, she developed a typology wherein she proposed four temperaments: meditative (thoughtful), spontaneous, executive, and social.

She and her daughter Isabel Briggs Myers developed a questionnaire, the Myers-Briggs Type Indicator, to show differing psychological preferences in how people perceive the world around them and make decisions. The concept was based on a theory proposed by Swiss psychiatrist Carl Jung who speculated that humans experience the world using four principal psychological functions—sensation, intuition, feeling, and thinking, and that one of these four functions is dominant for a person most of the time. Based on this research, there are sixteen types of personalities. In simple terms, we are types.

Every man I married was a type—real people with my expectations on them. When my expectations didn't unfold as I thought, my thinking was now what? Do I accept my decision as a final mistake or not? I wasn't going to create a Patricia Mills environment, with some guy being the Patricia.

What my mother meant to me was not having a choice but being a victim; I was born to her, and I had no opportunity to choose my mother, but I was no longer a victim. I was determined not to spend my life as a victim. Convinced life held so much more than what I experienced or was experiencing. God made victors, not victims!

# All My Exes Were Types

Names not used, as they are unnecessary, the types are the critical part to be remembered. I took no deliberate intent on choosing a mate, lacking an understanding of what a man should be and do. From every example of a man in my life, I could pull qualities I liked and disliked.

My grandfather was playful but mean. He fed his family but wasn't nurturing; He imparted no words of wisdom, insisting we come together for holidays and Sundays. As an adult, I questioned why was he there; was it that people of his generation didn't leave or divorce? Nevertheless, this was my grandfather, a playful yet mean character, all at the same time. He was my mother's first leader.

My father was a relaxed/nonchalant type of man till he consumed copious amounts of alcohol, becoming who he imagined himself to be or being who he was, which was it, I'm not sure. My father would say, "A drunk man speaks a sober mind," so I gathered alcohol was a type of liquid courage. The idea that drinking permitted something you wanted to do anyway seemed cowardly.

My oldest brother, only two years my senior, was a type. When he became involved with girls, he became another person; cared less for his siblings and more about his appearance. He would frequently change his clothes four times before leaving the house. He dressed well, and his fair complexion made him a ladies' man. I now understand he had no man's guidance. Our father wasn't available, and my grandfather wasn't an example to follow. None of our uncles were accessible to lend direction for him to be a man of integrity or wisdom.

All my uncles were types. I had two I saw often. The rest were in other states. My one uncle lived less than a block away, and he was a womanizer: never hiding what he found attractive in a woman he was lusting after. I remember feeling a little uncomfortable when I would hear my uncle commenting on a woman's body parts. He wasn't speaking of a lady with respect; it seemed measly, adding to my already indifferent impression of men.

He worked for Ford Motor Company, took care of his family, and was a sounding board for my mother. He once came to the house to check my oldest brother. I don't remember the details, but it involved him rebelling against my mother, which, given the environment's volatility, he may have. He just spoke with him. That was all he needed. My brother wasn't a fighter, he probably felt as I did "I can't wait to get out of Patricia Mills' house."

My other uncle lived on the westside of Detroit in a lovely home with his wife. He would come to pick up my siblings and me occasionally on Saturdays, at least the three youngest of us myself, my sister, and my youngest brother. Until he and his wife started having children. He was always kind, and I never witnessed this uncle talk under a woman's clothes. I never observed him angry, not even when I crashed this experimental pedal-powered vehicle. It was like a bike with additional seats. I turned too fast, tipping it over. He may have been angry, but he didn't let it show.

Then there was Mr. D, a neighbor. He was a family man, blue-collar worker. He took care of his house: cut the grass and kept his bushes trimmed well. He had one of the most well-manicured lawns on the street. He had three daughters and a wife. These girls came outside to play in their fenced backyard only. He worked every day. One day, they moved.

Oh, let me not forget the man right next door; he was a type of character; quiet man, never heard him raise his voice, wore a dashiki and a well-formed afro. He adopted his nephews and niece. It was a different family mixture; whether this couple was married, I don't remember. I somewhat sensed they weren't legally married (during those times, people used the term common-law marriage to add some civility to living together.)

In 1957, common-law marriage ended so that the living situation may have been a common-law marriage in the late sixties, early seventies. My mother befriended the lady, so we had the unfortunate event of having to spend time in their house, regrettable because these people had roaches, lots of them sometimes even in the refrigerator and the food they served.

We didn't have bugs in our house, so it seemed like a big deal. What I remember most about this guy was he would sit on the front porch, smoke a joint, and then play this large bongo drum for hours in the evenings during the summer. This man worked; I don't remember where. Eventually, this couple moved to a big house on Virginia Park, on the westside of Detroit. This house was perfect for that dramatic family of eight.

## My Family, the Neighbors, and Friends Make Impression

My impression of family and life was shaped and formed by my family, neighbors, and friends. My mother had few friends since she was sick, most of the time, she couldn't hold a job. My aunts served as her friends and occasionally a neighbor, none of whom lived there for long.

However briefly they lived there, they all brought an impression, a shaping value with their temporary interaction that I remember. I observed how the presence of adults, whoever they were, affected by my mother's behavior; it was as if she transformed into another person.

## CHAPTER 20

# 34 Years of Jailing and Petty Politics

My daily routine was to ride my bike at lunchtime, but on this day, my afternoon break was interrupted by the captain of Internal Affairs, summoning me for an interview. I contacted my prayer partner and went to the meeting.

On July 31, 2019, at eleven o'clock, I was interviewed by Internal Affairs for my last lousy marriage to Ekong, which happened thirteen years earlier. The line of questioning was to make my relationship current (I kept thinking, what is the meaning of this?) with my ex-husband, the dead man.

All I felt was embarrassment during this interview. I believed somebody when I shouldn't have. The unsaid standard was that a cop knows a criminal, but cops are not supermen (though some may think they are). They don't have x-ray vision. The captain started with the had fifteen aliases Ekong had, which I replied, "How would I know that? I couldn't run him in LEIN." She said that's not the only way to find out about a person (never elaborating on how).

The first question was, "Did you make a notification?" I responded, "I don't remember; I believe I did." *That was thirteen years ago!* The captain and sergeant stated they could find out if I had. I asked them, "Did you know I notified the federal government about this guy's nefarious activities in the Ford Building?"

From the look on their faces, I knew they were oblivious to that detail in their investigation. Clearly, this stack of papers the captain brought in the room was mostly, if not all, department computer-generated papers. The captain immediately asked me, "Well, did you make notification of your conversation with the feds?" Make a notification of a conversation with a law enforcement agency to report a crime? I didn't know I had to! I stated to the captain. "I met with them in Jail Division Two in the lieutenant's office, so the department knew."

I attempted to explain to these interviewers I don't remember my courtships. I had been married three times. I don't recall wedding dates and don't remember divorce dates; it's not like it's a time to celebrate; if I overthink it, I would be depressed. I refused to live my life holding onto past mistakes. I don't talk to any of my ex's, what's the point of that activity, they're all dead relationships.

For three hours, this captain and sergeant questioned me about this mistake I made, and most of my answers were "I don't remember," and that appeared to mount their frustration toward me. At one point, the captain slid me a box of tissues that I rejected; I was embarrassed, not scared.

The sergeant said, "You need to give us something, help us, help you." I thought, are you serious? I repeatedly told them, "I don't remember." Internal affairs don't help anybody but themselves; these people look to burn others to lift themselves.

I had nothing to hide. Yes, I was stupid, but I was guilty of no crime or departmental violation. This policy was from 2008 and my marriage to this character was in 2006. In 2006 you made notification, but getting permission wasn't a factor under the previous system; that policy allowed the officer to operate at their discretion, which is the way it should be. The current administration wasn't in place when this policy was drafted.

The captain said to me, "Well, sergeant, if you don't tell us something, I'm going to have to pull out these papers" I thought go ahead do it, but I said, "What do you want me to say? I don't remember." She showed me pictures of him and the legal documents of the marriage and divorce. I acknowledged them, "Yes, all that looks familiar."

After a line of questioning failed to establish the relationship was current or started in the jail, which would've made me in violation of the undersheriff 2008 policy for fraternization, I kept thinking, where is this coming from? I sat there embarrassed by this wrong decision I made. The same questions seem to last forever. Around one o'clock, the sergeant asked me did I have sex with this guy when he was locked up in the county, which I stated, "No, I didn't know this man when he was in the county jail, and no I didn't visit him in prison." He said, "Well, according to the work assignments, you should've known him." I responded, "He and several other inmates. You can't tell me what I should remember."

Not meaning to come across as sarcastic, but I was frustrated. This whole ordeal that was thirteen years old. The captain had me read policies and followed that with the questions of didn't you violate that policy. I told her, "I made notifications, I don't remember to who? That was thirteen years ago."

The sergeant asked me, "Well, when was the last time you spoke to him?" I replied, "I don't remember." He said, "Well, you need to remember." I was thinking, why? As if I committed some awful murder, this was an incident that wasn't a violation at that time. I couldn't believe this line of questions. I told them, "I think when he got out of federal prison, some years ago." The sergeant said when was that? I told him I didn't remember. Again, he said, "You need to remember," but I repeated I didn't know. In frustration, I said, "I don't remember, what do you want me to do, make up something for you?" They both quickly said, "No." I asked them is this about me leaving (meaning retiring). She (the captain) just stared at me as the sergeant asked politely, "Do you want to leave?" I said no.

We broke for ten minutes break, where I briefly spoke with my union rep. Upon reconvening, the captain says to me, "You're a woman, and I can't believe you don't remember." I just looked at her, thinking, what do you people want from me, and honestly, what does that mean?

By this time, the rejected box of tissue came in handy. I couldn't believe what was happening! I worked with both of these people during my thirty-four years. Now for some reason, I became the bad guy. As the captain sat her pin down, the sergeant asked me one final question he said, "Don't you feel better now that you talked to us? You had to know one day you were going have to talk to us." I replied, "No, because I know I made notification," and in frustration, I told them, "I ain't scare of y'all." I couldn't believe I said that to IA, with their reputation, everybody fears them. I didn't view them as I would have several years earlier, but now I knew my worth in Christ Jesus, I fear God, not men!

I respected these people, but I didn't fear them. These were men sitting across the table from me. That day, my faith in Christ Jesus spoke, and it scared me because speaking up like that wasn't the accepted norm during an interview of that type. I couldn't apologize, nor did I want to apologize for the boldness that came out of my mouth. I went into that interview confident God was with me; I came out bold. I would not have said that had the sergeant refrained from asking me that ridiculous question. Who do these people think they are, gods? It didn't matter; they are not my God.

The captain then concluded the meeting, requested my badge and identification and stated, "This was just a tip, and I had to do due diligence." Whatever that meant and further said, "I will see what I can do about your position," as if what took place in that meeting was personal. My position was a non-gun carrying function. I didn't need my gun for my daily assignment.

When I returned to the jail that afternoon, my prayer partner and I prayed again, and we asked Father God for sudden revelation in Jesus' name.

The next morning, I received a text from a friend about the Duncan V. Wayne County Detroit case in the Detroit News. The personal situation between Peter Duncan, his finance, and the undersheriff was in the Michigan Supreme Court. As I read that article, I could see the questions asked of me came because of this case. I still couldn't figure out why this? Why now? Perhaps it was time to go.

But before I did that, I needed to be sure this was God's best for me. Sure, I was bored and wanted to do something else, but I wasn't sure what that was. A part of my daily prayers was thanking Jesus for my new position.

When I returned to work on Monday, my new assignment was to an officer floor security position (center station), essentially demoted. I called the sheriff's secretary to get an appointment with the sheriff, was told he would be out of town for the next three weeks. The running joke was the sheriff's in Florida. I received no return phone call for an appointment.

After three days of being a floor security officer, my demotion by a tip, I fasted and prayed with my prayer partner. The fasting was for me to hear Father God speak, I'm sure he was talking to me all the while, but I kept telling myself I needed do one more thing that required cash, basically not trusting God. Now that I was thinking about it, and with convincing myself it's not so bad here. It wasn't just unsatisfactory; it was terrible, like being in a bad relationship. I loved some of the people there, but I was at end of the road. All the while praying for a position Father God has designed for me.

Weeks before this event, I was meditating on the books of Esther and Daniel, they sought God by fasting and praying. In this situation, it may seem obvious what to do, but I did the apparent too many times, and I was incorrect in that assertion. Once the fast was over, I had peace with retiring as much as I didn't want too. As one of my friends put it best, "Sarge, how much longer are you planning to work at that godawful place?" That question prompted me to wonder and evaluate this situation.

The money was good, but the environment was toxic. Now, without the insulation of leaving the building for lunch. Being demoted to a floor security officer, I was feeling a little stressed by this situation. It was sobering. I was a thirty-four-year veteran. Was this the best I could receive in my last days at Wayne County? I went to the Wayne County Retirement Department. It was time to leave. The day I signed my papers: I prayed and signed with peace.

The reality of what I would be fighting for sat in: I would be battling to stay in a toxic environment, where sixteen hours was a workday, write-ups were commonplace. Working consecutive doubles made you prone to mistakes due to lack of rest. I would be fighting to stay in a place where I now had to bring toilet paper, scot towel, and soap to use the restroom. I would be struggling to stay in a place where now I was a target from past mistakes.

For the past twelve years, I watched the present administration take police powers from mostly officers of color. Then, right before the two-year mark of losing their certification, give it back only to turn around in six months, and retake it. I was sure fighting wasn't something I wanted to do. After evaluating, I realize it was more insane to stay than to leave.

This was spiritual, a spiritual battle that wasn't mine, it's the Lord's (2 Chronicles 20:15 and 1 Samuel 17:47). God fights for his people, and I belong to the Lord Jesus. My position was to feed on God's word, and he would protect me and guide me.

For two consecutive weeks, my Joseph Prince app delivered sermons to me during this challenging time: Win the Battle Over Hopelessness and Answers for Dark Nights & Difficult Seasons. Both sermons seem to speak directly to me; Jesus loves me! He was speaking to me during this difficult time. Father God was guiding and keeping me.

God provided me with lights along this transition to pray with and for me: a friend to confirm and support, a friend to guide me in administration matters, and an exceptional friend to make me laugh. Being a person used to getting up and going to work was an intricate part of this transition. God gave me another assignment. My morning meditation and scripture reading prepared me for the next step, Father God had for me. Plus, now I could make my morning workouts my routine again.

God's grace is in my every thought when my mind is stayed on Him (Jeremiah 26:3). One day I was at work, complaining to the Lord about some person, I don't remember who or about what and the Lord said, "I love them too." That changed my complaining permanently. It wasn't scripture that arrested my complaining, but God dealing with me right in that moment. This isn't to say reading God's word isn't necessary. Quite the contrary, because I enjoy reading the Bible, He's always speaking to me, He and His word are one.

When it was time to leave Wayne County, God's grace was working. The month my retirement was official, reports of the pandemic were steadily increasing. God removed me from the jails, a nasty environment where the transient population of society frequently visited because of their lifestyle decisions.

## CHAPTER 21

# Divine Intervention? Blessing in Disguise

For the last couple of years, I was petitioning Father God for a position, not just a job. I was bored with Wayne County and their administrative meanies. Pastor Joseph Prince, who I began listening to in 2011, said in one of his sermons, "Don't ask God for a job, ask God for a position." Hence, I began to claim my position.

I sensed I was done with the sheriff's office, and I felt I went as far as I could go. The mismanagement makes employees overworked and underpaid, which makes for a place operating daily on low morale. How can you be kind when you get four to five hours of sleep per day? It's a form of modern-day slavery.

Was all this a blessing in disguise? Days after deciding to retire, I saw the jail environment in a way I couldn't see before. My lunchtime bike rides insulated me from the harshness and toxicity of the situation. Deputies had to buy chairs for duty. At the end of their shift, it's like watching musical chairs. You can't work sixteen hours in a lousy chair; a wrong chair equals an injured back.

## All Authority Is Ordained by God

Police officers are one profession mentioned in the Bible. In Romans 13:1–4 says, "The authority of the government invests police officers with powers; God appoints that authority. Therefore, resistance is resistance to God's ordinance, and those who resist will bring judgement to themselves. For rulers are not a terror to good works, but evil. To be unafraid of the authority, do what is good, and you will have praise of the same. For he is God's ministers to you for good. But if you do evil, be afraid: for he does not bear the sword in vain: for he is God ministers to you for good. But if you do wrong, be afraid, for he is God's minister, an avenger to execute wrath on him who practices evil."

In 1 Timothy 2:1–2 God says by supplication, prayers, intercessions, and giving of thanks be made for all men for kings and all that are in authority, that we lead a quiet and peaceable life in all godliness and reverence. The government and those in service need prayer. In my youth, I thought police officers, and the government served the people, and perhaps I did because the Detroit Public School system taught that. Maybe I was supposed to be in ministry, just not this ministry.

I genuinely love and care about people. I possess a sense of justice; I think in terms of black and white, right and wrong, but law enforcement or corrections isn't about right and wrong. It's more about politics and budgetary matters. The world is full of hurting people, and as a law enforcement officer, you don't help people, you follow the rules. Once a person reaches the jail, they still can't be supported by an officer. As an officer, your conduct is professionalism; everything is professional, not personal. Still, the people you're meeting are hurting from the making of their own or someone else's. Either way as an officer, you can't help people in that capacity.

## CHAPTER 22

# My Valley Moment

Father God protected me and kept me during those times. I call that my Psalm 23:4 moment. I let myself in that valley. Not that he approved, but that I am his and he loves me, whether I am right or wrong in action. I am in Jesus Christ. He is my Lord and Savior and that's how Father God sees me then and now. It's Jesus Christ that made me righteous and cleanses me. The Bible says if we walk in the light as He is in the light; we have fellowship with one another, and the blood of Jesus Christ, His Son, cleanses us from all sin (I John 1:7).

It's this cleansing that kept me in the light, not of my works, bringing me to the redeeming quality of graciousness. God hates sin because sin destroys, not because he doesn't want you having fun. Sin robs you of God's wholeness he has for you, which is far better than the temporary satisfaction of a moment of sin.

## How Can You Lose Your Salvation When It's Based on the Blood of Jesus?

Contrary to what most churches teach, you can't lose your salvation. My salvation is locked in the finished works at the cross by the blood of Jesus, not my accomplishments. If it's based on my doings, it isn't worth much, but it's all based on Jesus' finished works at the cross, and that's never going to change. Neither is my salvation ever lost; it's by His blood, not mine, his finished works. My salvation is based on the eternal works of Jesus Christ on the cross. Jesus Christ did the deeds that set me free!

Having said that, I must say you can't escape the consequences of your wayward decisions. Honestly, why would you want to sin against a loving Father, because that's who God is! Knowing how much God loves me makes me want to talk about him all the time to whoever will listen. Knowing how much God loves me makes me want to please him, not because I'm afraid I'll lose his approval. According to scripture, Jesus Christ is the same yesterday, today and forever (Hebrews 13:8).

The Father and the Son are one. John 10:30 says that love God has is in effect when I sin. My sin isn't more potent than the love of God or the blood of Jesus Christ. The consciousness that Father God loves me and that Jesus Christ finished works on the cross is my righteousness. It keeps me from falling into condemnation (Romans 8:1). There is now no condemnation to them that are in Christ Jesus, when falling short. I'm going to miss the mark no matter what my best efforts are. And if I could do better, why would Jesus need to come? Because we can't do better! We do better when we see more of Jesus!

## The Law versus Grace

Why do we, the church, discount the blood of the Lord Jesus Christ by teaching we can lose our salvation? That teaching is the law, not grace. The covenant between Jonathan and David in 1 Samuel 18:3 can't be more significant than the bond we have with Christ Jesus. Jesus died for us. Jonathan loved David as his soul, 1 Samuel 18:1. When Jonathan died in battle, David mourned for Jonathan and King Saul 2 Samuel 1:17.

As King, David remembered his covenant with Jonathan in 2 Samuel 9 and fetched his son Mephibosheth from Lo-debar. When he arrived at David, he fell on his face in reverence and obedience. David said, "Mephibosheth." He answered, "Behold your servant!" David said to him "Fear not: for I will shew you kindness for Jonathan, thy father's sake and will restore thee all the land of Saul, thy father;

and thou shalt eat bread at my table." Now this man, Mephibosheth, bowed himself and said, "What is thy servant, that thou shouldest look upon such a dead dog as I am?"

## Our Relationship with God in Christ Jesus Typology

At that moment, Mephibosheth is like the believer that doesn't know his position in Christ Jesus. King David wasn't honoring him in his own right or something he had done, but because of the relationship David had with his father, Jonathan. Father God keeps the believer, because of Christ Jesus, not because of anything he has done or could do; it's all about the finished works of Jesus Christ at the cross.

The relationship between two men, not God and man, but this man, King David, remembered a covenant with his covenant partner and was moved to honor him by showing kindness to his surviving relative. King David didn't care this man couldn't walk; it wasn't the condition of the relative that made him valuable it was the relationship the king had with his father, Jonathan, that gave Mephibosheth a position at the king's table.

Why do we think God will do less than the man he created? God said David was a man after my heart, which shall fulfill all my will (Acts 13:22). The creation can't be higher than the creator: we were created in his image, in his likeness (Gen. 1:26). Nothing about man is original. Our idea of a covenant pales in comparison. King David's compassion moved him to honor a surviving relative of his covenant partner. That act was like our Father God. Why do we think less of the Father? Won't God honor us by blessing our house, because of our position in Christ Jesus?

In 2 Samuel 7:29, God bestowed a servant King David; we are sons under a new covenant in Christ Jesus. The Abrahamic covenant promises righteousness by faith (Gen. 15:6 and Rom. 4:3). King David was a man that loved God but took the wife of one of his brave men, slept with her, and impregnated her. Then, in an attempt to cover his sin, summoned for her husband, Uriah. When Uriah refused to sleep in comfort while his men were on the battlefield,

King David had the man murdered. Uriah, a man of valor, hand delivered his death notice to Joab, second in charge to King David (2 Samuel 11:1–15). Yes, King David repented, and God gave him Solomon (2 Samuel 12:1–25).

What a good God! God is merciful. So again, why do we believe He's not? I think it's because most local churches teach a mixture of law and grace. Because it's a belief that the Ten Commandments are more excellent than Jesus Christ, that's not true. If that was so, Jesus Christ didn't need to come and die for us!

## The Dividing Line Is a Consciousness of Christ Jesus

I proclaimed the goodness of the Lord wherever I would go, to whoever would. In claiming his love and faithfulness to his children, speaking about Jesus Christ brings me joy, and contentment beyond what words can express. That is the state that divided me from my colleagues and insulated me all my years of service at The Wayne County Sheriff's Office. Enyi was right; I'm not like my partners. I know my Father, God loves me, and that makes a world of difference in a place of negative influences and departmental challenges.

## CHAPTER 23

# 2014: Visit to Abuja, Nigeria

In 2014, I went to visit Enyi in Abuja, Nigeria. For me, it was more of an opportunity to see the Niger River, a historic place that runs through Abuja. According to a few books I read, the first slaves kidnapped from Africa were taken captive from up the Niger River.

When I arrived and made it through customs, one of the uniform men asked me, "Who are you here with, or are you meeting someone?" I thought, okay, I better not get comfortable here! No one has ever asked me that upon arrival and by him asking me that meant something, and by God's grace, I wasn't going to find out why.

Abuja had no museums, which is one thing I took for granted would be there. Enyi took me to Gurara Falls. I took lots of pictures of the falls. They were beautiful. In fact, everywhere I went, he took me. Whether this was a courtesy or safety concern, I'm not sure.

The Niger River was at low tide at that time of year. The river rose and fall depending on the season. In January, it was shallow and the bridge Enyi and I were standing on made him nervous. It looked as if it required repair. But I thought it's okay; cars were traveling, and people were walking on it. But at his nervousness, we got off that bridge.

In America, if a bridge isn't safe, it's taken out of use, and a detour is made around that bridge until repairs occur. There is a public safety standard in America, a measure not held around the world. I observed trash everywhere in bags, as well as loose; it reminded me of Ecuador. Whether these two countries: Abuja and Ecuador, had a public works or sanitation department, I don't know.

Traveling taught me to appreciate America. The little things that once bothered me became nonexistent. Sure, we pay a lot of taxes, but I am grateful for my trash being picked up weekly, and most roads are safe. Enyi explained to me that the people that lived around the river are the ancestors of the previous generations; there is very little migration. I was thinking so; this would be like the third or fourth generation of the Atlantic slave trade era families that lived around the river. They didn't appear to be living well.

On my way back to the hotel, I thought I'd take a dip in the pool. The brochure and internet advertised the location had a pool, so I got dressed to get some pool time, only to be told by the desk clerk, "Oh, the pool's not up yet." I thought, are you kidding! I asked no more questions simply because it was evident it was just a scam to get people there (the area was closed off, and no one was working on it).

Since I was only going to be there a few more days, what difference was it going to make? Why fuss or require a refund on my room because the accommodations weren't as advertised? If this were an American hotel, I would have, but when I visit other countries, I don't anything; after all, I'm in their country, regardless of what they promise by the brochure. I don't return to that hotel or recommend it to anyone else. If I return to that country, I find another hotel.

There was a church near the hotel, but I didn't attend it. I wondered why they had church service every day. The Bible says in Acts 2:46, believers met daily in the temple. So I was familiar with the idea of daily church, but I certainly wasn't going alone or uninvited. I asked Enyi when he came to see me, why was that church meeting every day he told me, "That's what they do here, go to church every day." I asked so they are really into the Bible. He said, "No, it's a social thing." I thought, okay, thinking about a few things I experienced with Ekong.

By nature, I'm curious, but I wasn't going to venture out in that land. Everywhere I went, Enyi took me, and I also didn't talk, not that he told me not to. I just felt I shouldn't. I enjoy talking with the local people when I traveled, but Abuja was different. It wasn't like Hong Kong or Japan or Ecuador; the energy was like no other place I had ever been before!

It was a pleasant traveling experience, and I was happy to see my old friend again, but I knew it would be a while if ever I returned to Nigeria. I learned more about the people by visiting than I would've ever learned by reading a book. A book is one person's opinion of a place, time, or people. It's a guess why people do the things they do or did. It was something about being there that spoke volumes to my soul.

My introduction at the airport was a warning of sorts that I heeded. The cop in me was on duty; the questions people ask are often indicators of threat assessment. The airport had few concessions stands, and no souvenir stands. That may not seem like much, but my thinking was the small concession and souvenirs shop worker give you a vibe of how the people are. But the uniform guy gave a vibe of better watch yourself here, you're not safe!

Had I visited Abuja before I met Ekong or Nkem, I wouldn't have steered clear of both of them. Not because everyone there is terrible, but because of the differences in thinking. He viewed credit as free money; it's not. It is a promissory note that you must pay at a later day, with interest.

That mentality in America means lousy credit for them or someone that trusts them, because they see no need to pay once they get what they want. Not understanding credit is a money problem waiting to happen. Nothing destroys a marriage or relationship quicker than money issues.

I thought since Nigeria was a part of OPEC countries; the country was affluent, as were the people, but I was wrong, the people are poor. The land is fertile with resources, but the funds are in the hands of a few. The people of that country appear to exist to survive. My visit to that place opened my understanding of the poverty of that country. At the same time, it still maintains a position in OPEC industries that speaks of government corruption. Enyi would say, "The United States was a whore country," but I didn't take him seriously. He was speaking his value system.

My youth was fascinated by his charm, he knew scripture, and we talked about the Bible all the time, but what I didn't realize was the Bible—God's word wasn't in his heart, and he didn't know Jesus, he knew his words, not the man. He taught me just because you know the stories in the Bible doesn't mean you know Jesus.

Upon departing from Nigeria, I remember thinking this was the land where my ancestor was retrieved? No, I can't entirely agree with the method by which my ancestors got ripped from the soil: kidnapped, stole, or sold to end up in America. It was an atrocity that landed my people in American, a land that freed its slaves long after slavery was still a common practice in Nigeria. I am truly glad I was born in America, especially being a woman.

## CHAPTER 24

# God and Father God's Love in Demonstration

God loved Israel so much. He rose Moses to deliver them from bondage (Exodus 3:10); God sent plagues and instructed Israel to protect themselves from being affected by the epidemics meant for their captors (Exodus 7:12). Once they were released, He parted the Red Sea (Exodus 14:13–16) and fed them in the wilderness. Imagine that! In the desert, where there is no water, God provided. When the food they had from Egypt ran out, God provided (Exodus 16:15). Israel complained about flesh. God gave them flesh lots of it (Numbers 11:18–20).

When I read and listened, it gave a visional effect to something I heard plenty of times. But now, the visional gave emotions to the hearing and seeing. God was no longer this far away figure, unable to be touched by my human emotions. He is our Heavenly Father. When God became alive, that affected my relationship with God. He became a person with emotions, a physical being, Jesus Christ. Yet even with this revelation, I felt I needed to make myself better. Still not grasping what Jesus Christ had done at the cross.

## Wrong Thinking and Bad Application

As a single parent, I would occasionally permit myself to make offerings to the Church, not tithe. Why? I needed to provide for my children. Yeah, I attended church on Sunday. Malachi 3:8–10 says, "Will a man rob God? Yet ye robbed me, even this whole nation. Bring all the tithes into the storehouse, and prove me now herewith, saith the Lord of host, if I will not open you the windows of heaven, and pour you out a blessing, that there shall not be room enough to receive it." Every time I went to church, it didn't come alive until I sought God in my bible study time.

God is so awesome, and in all his awesomeness, he says "Prove me." I thought, God, how you can be so excellent and still tell us to prove you? In other words, He says, allow me to show you (this is the creator of Heaven and Earth saying, give me a chance). The book of Malachi was written to the children of Israel (God's chosen people), not the church; the church didn't come to be till the death, burial, and resurrection of Jesus Christ. For years, I heard Malachi 3:8–10 during offering collection time, felt convicted, and wasn't sure why.

When the Holy Spirit introduced me to the ministry of Pastor Joseph Prince, rightly dividing the word came into understanding. The whole Bible is for me, the believer, but not directed to me, meaning not all of it, is for the believer. In the Old Testament, you see the heart of God, and in the New Testament, you can see the manifestation of God's love in Christ Jesus. Throughout the Bible, you can find Jesus in the old covenant. He's revealed in typology and the new covenant, He is the Son of God.

## Still, What Is My Purpose?

My relationship with God required a constant fellowship, and I grew to the point of taking some things for granted. I stop listening, but still attended church, bored in the way of like I was playing church. Playing church, but always returning the tithe (I knew enough to know the tithe belongs to the Lord), but I was asking God, so now what? I ceased seeking God's will for my life and pursued my way.

What is my purpose in God's grand scheme of things? With my girls getting older, it appeared that my goal there was completed. I began to wonder what I should be doing with my time. Go back to school? I thought to finish my second degree, but I didn't want another degree in criminal justice. Besides, once I left Wayne County, I felt no more police work for me. So, I went to the Labor School at Wayne State University. I learned about the labor movement since I was a union steward. I began to understand that this union business stuff wasn't for me either. The unions came into existence to provide workplace equality, but that's not what was happening on the executive board of Sheriff's Local 502; it seemed everyone was out for themselves. The union was another good idea gone bad.

I was restless. In hindsight, it was a time to seek direction from God, not attempt to find my way. I read Stephen R. Covey's book, The 7 Habits of Highly Effective People, attended seminars for self-improvement with Franklin-Covey. The first was "Focus: Achieving Your Highest Priorities," this seminar focused on prioritizing your life. The second was "The 7 Habits of Highly Effective Managers," that seminar concentrated on managing your life in a way to achieve your desired result. I incorporated the Franklin Planner in my life. I thought these books and seminars prepared me for my next steps. I developed the habit of reviewing my thoughts daily and weekly. I was meditating on myself instead of God's word. I replaced it with intellectual reasoning, studying myself. Not God's best.

I was taking my focus off Him and putting it on me. The morning was my quiet time. At 4:00 a.m. I started my work-out and meditation, which consisted of listening to Bible-based VHS tapes to get some form of Word first thing in the morning. It became a routine void of spiritual quality. Running on my stair-stepper for an hour, so I was physically fit, but spiritually dull. The Bible-based tapes I would listen to while working out were Old Testament based, meaning there was no highlighting Jesus Christ and His finished works at the cross. I was looking to the law, not grace, which made me dull spiritually. On my quest to evolve, I learned about other companies that offered seminars.

These seminars were more toward professional conduct. "How to Become a Better Communicator," "The Essentials of Communicating with Diplomacy and Professionalism," "The Essentials of Credibility, Composure, and Confidence," and my favorite and most fitting for my workplace "Overcoming Workplace Negativity." Attending these seminars offered professional and personal development because it put me in an environment with professionals looking to elevate their careers with proper workplace etiquette. Again, I was on information overload.

None provided wisdom because that comes from Father God. The shortcut to professional success is to look to Jesus. I failed to spend the necessary time before my Heavenly Father for His direction for my life. I had compartmentalized Father God. Too often, I heard from well-meaning people that God isn't going to tell you everything to do, what to wear, or what to eat for lunch. I now know, He will!

All I needed to do was stay tuned to the channel of the Holy Word. There is a story for every occasion and circumstance. Since God is the same throughout His Word, you see His heart for them that seek Him. I neglected to develop my spirit in God's things in the pursuit of man's reasoning. I was attending seminars and reading self-help books that only left me bored spiritually, but intellectually, informed. Had I taken the time to build my confidence in God's things, marriage number three would not have happened the way it happened. Still not ready.

## ❧ CHAPTER 25 ❧

# *Apologies*

The event deeply affected Harold. He called me one day and said, "I'm sorry about your hands, you were just standing there, you weren't playing with matches, I was." His apology was a big deal because my big brother doesn't apologize! This incident was obviously on his mind and heart for a while, and it must've taken a lot to call me and apologize.

I appreciated it, but I never blamed him; we were children, and I didn't remember I wasn't playing with fire but standing there watching him. It didn't matter; we were all victims. I told him it wasn't his fault, Momma burned me. She was supposed to love and nurture us, not abuse us. We were her children. I welcomed the conversation as it was the first of its kind that acknowledged what happened and how I received the burns. It was like the elephant in the room; everybody knew it was there, but no one dared mention it for fear of reprisal from our mother.

Before having this conversation with my oldest brother, I never thought much about how my hands affected my siblings, but it did. I realized it may have made my little sister to avoid being a victim. My youngest brother was fretful; just as our mother told me I was unwanted; she did the same to him. My oldest brother shouldered the burden and responsibility of taking care of all of us when my mother fell sick (kidney or bladder infections, a host of other physical and mental health issues).

He cooked, cleaned, and helped her write checks. He paid the cost of repeating the third grade, holding us together as a family. He was my mother's delegated assistant as firstborn. That conversation with my brother was the catalyst for me asking my mother for an apology.

## My Mother's Apology

I was thirty-five years old when my mother eventually apologized for burning me. That personal discharge seemed to fix my thoughts about my mother. She appeared to be genuinely sorry for burning my hands, and that was enough for me. My relationship with my mother held a special place in my heart. The apology gave me a new beginning. Sure, she would still do things that rubbed me the wrong way. But I believed her expression of regret came from a real place, not a place of perfection but humbleness.

As difficult as it was to ask her for an apology for burning my hands. At thirty-five years old, I realize I needed to hear her apologize. Not tell me why, because it was apparent! There was no reason to rehash that painful place in the past. She immediately began to cry and told me she knew I was having problems with this issue. She said, "I'm sorry," still not mentioning hands or the burns. Perhaps it was too painful for her to say, "I'm sorry, or I apologize for burning your hands." Her sorry and tears were enough; we never talked about it again.

She made me a quilt of mud cloth, unlike anything I ever saw, except maybe in a museum. It is beautiful and took her years to collect the pieces. When she presented it to me, she also made a matching pillow. That was her way of apologizing.

When I was working for the county, my mother would call me every day when I was at work. She always started with, "How's your day going?" Whether or not things were going well, I always said good. I didn't want her to worry about something that was out of both our control. Our conversations would mostly involve her just talking about her neighbors and what they were doing. She came to a place where, before we hung up that she would say she loved me.

I never took that for granted because I prayed for years to hear her say those words. I know God answers prayers, not just mine, all the righteous ones. The prayer of the righteous man avails much (James 5:16).

# Rite of Passage

My mother's transition woke a new reality in me: it wasn't what my mother would say, but who she was! The elevated position of mother is irreplaceable. It can't be compared to any other relationship, though frequently compared to our divine connection with our Heavenly Father. The family I was born into wasn't a mistake. God placed me there and equipped me, gave me divine favor with my Aunt Audrey. The Bible sitting on the living room coffee table and my love for reading are gifts from God. The living word of God caused me to call out to Him, as a child when my mother was having conniptions. The Bible, just being there was a saving grace.

After several divorces, I realized relationships work like a buffer when making decisions. The first factor in making a decision is what Father God saying, not well-meaning friends and family. Let God's voice be the authoritative voice in decision making. Marriage works with three parties working in concert: the man, Jesus Christ, and the woman. Living examples aren't governing the influences of marriage and family. Basing decisions on my ideas always got me into places I didn't want to be. Jesus Christ is the way, the truth, and the life (John 14:16). Simplify your life, follow Jesus Christ!

# Salvation Prayer

Lord Jesus,

Thank you for loving me and dying for me on the cross. Your precious blood has washed me clean of every sin. I believe You rose from the dead and are alive today. You are my Lord and Savior now and forever. Because of Your finished works at the cross, I am now a beloved child of God. Heaven is my home. Thank You for giving me eternal life and filling my heart with Your love, joy, and peace.

Amen

# About the Author

Grace Mills is a survivor of child abuse delivered by the hand of God to live her worth. She believes her life journey is to be a witness to the love of Jesus Christ.

She is a follower of Jesus Christ, a member of Faith Xperience Church in Detroit, MI, and a partner of Joseph Prince Ministries. The partnership with Joseph Prince ministries, and Grace's desire to see more of Jesus, influenced her to travel to Singapore and Israel.

Grace is a mother of two beautiful daughters, one awesome son-in-love, and three adorable grandchildren.

She is a retired police sergeant from the Wayne County Sheriff's Office in the city of Detroit, where she served for 34 years.

CPSIA information can be obtained
at www.ICGtesting.com
Printed in the USA
BVHW071709030122
625370BV00006B/164

9 781644 682838